*Controlling Technocracy:*
*Citizen Rationality and the Nimby Syndrome*

# Controlling Technocracy: Citizen Rationality and the Nimby Syndrome

*Gregory E. McAvoy*

GEORGETOWN UNIVERSITY PRESS / WASHINGTON, D.C.

Georgetown University Press, Washington, D.C. 20007
©1999 by Georgetown University Press, All rights reserved.
Printed in the United States of America
10  9  8  7  6  5  4  3  2  1  1999

Library of Congress Cataloging-in-Publication Data

McAvoy, Gregory E.
    Controlling technocracy : citizen rationality and the Nimby
syndrome / Gregory E. McAvoy.
        p.  cm. — (American governance and public policy)
    Includes bibliographical references and index.
    ISBN 0-87840-740-5 (cloth). — ISBN 0-87840-741-3 (pbk.)
    1. NIMBY syndrome—United States.  2. Land use—Government policy-
-United States—Citizen participation.  3. Science and state—United
States—Citizen participation.  4. Technology and state—United
States—Citizen participation.  I. Title.  II. Series.
HD205.M36  1999                                        99-18787
333.73'13'0973—DC21                                    CIP

*for my mom,*
*Ruth McAvoy*

*and to the memory of my dad,*
*Ken McAvoy*

# Contents

# *Preface*

The Nimby syndrome is a relatively new term in the lexicon of social scientists, but the controversy surrounding it is rooted in a longstanding debate about the appropriate role of experts and citizens in policymaking. The tension between technocratic and democratic decision-making has occupied political thinkers as far back as Plato and Aristotle and has been addressed more recently by prominent social scientists like Max Weber, Robert Dahl, and Charles Lindblom. The question continues to challenge us as the size and scope of government expands and as bureaucrats are armed with an ever larger set of tools for decision-making, from cost benefit analysis to public opinion surveys to environmental impact studies to long-term forecasting methods. As technical expertise grows, supporters of democratic decision-making must work harder to justify a role for citizens.

Although this book focuses on the tension between technocracy and democracy in the context of hazardous waste policy, the debate over the merits of technocracy and democracy also figures prominently in a variety of other policy areas. One that has generated a lot of controversy is the regulation of risks. This issue crosses a number of policy arenas from environmental hazards to second-hand smoke to passenger restraints in motor vehicles. Among the notable proponents of technocratic decision-making in this arena is Supreme Court Justice Stephen Breyer, who published his book on the pathologies of risk regulation, *Breaking the Vicious Circle*, shortly before his appointment to the Supreme Court. Interestingly, economic policy—the political problem that seems to occupy the minds of most voters—is one area where technocratic power is clearly ascendant. Stockholders, bond traders, politicians, and citizens wait in eager anticipation for the next pronouncement by Alan Greenspan so that they can know where the economy is headed. There is very little debate about curbing the Fed's power and a growing acquiescence to technocratic decision-making in this arena.

The focus of this book—hazardous waste siting—also poses a challenge for democratic governance that is increasingly common in contemporary policy debates: adjudicating between the interests of particular communities and more general interests. The difficulty of equitably choosing among particular and general interests is evident in a variety of siting decisions, from disposal facilities to halfway houses to airports. As people become more sensitized to environmental risks and perceived threats, we must figure out ways to fairly resolve conflicts between the general and particular interests of citizens. Some of the innovative solutions to siting described here can help stimulate thinking about ways to resolve such conflicts.

I first encountered many of these issues head-on in graduate seminars taught by John Freeman at the University of Minnesota. John consistently challenged us to understand not just the policy debates that we were studying but the implications that arose from them for democratic governance. In particular, he asked us to think about the extent to which we trusted policy analysts to make decisions for us on issues like foreign trade, health policy, and industrial policy and to see how this issue of trust or faith in experts was at the bottom of many of the debates about policymaking. In addition to guiding me toward interesting questions, John was a valuable advisor to me in the first incarnation of this project when it was my dissertation.

Also at the University of Minnesota, Larry Jacobs served as an important mentor in the dissertation writing stage, especially by pressing me to construct an argument that would be of interest to a wide audience. He continues to be a much-valued supporter. John Sullivan provided important encouragement and guidance, particularly in the development and analysis of the survey.

In addition, I owe a great deal of thanks to the Center for Urban and Regional Affairs (CURA) at the University of Minnesota. CURA provided a grant that allowed me to conduct the two public opinion surveys and to travel to Red Lake and Koochiching Counties to interview county residents. I would like to thank the residents of those two counties who agreed to meet and talk with me (and occasionally feed me). I am also grateful to the many Minnesota state officials and legislators who agreed to be interviewed or provided me with written materials. The Minnesota Office of Environmental Assistance provided many important documents that were critical to understanding the development of Minnesota's hazardous waste policy once the state abandoned its siting effort.

Of those outside of Minnesota who contributed to this project, Barry Rabe clearly stands at the top of the list. In his careful reading and re-reading of this manuscript, he provided many insightful questions, key substantive information, and some timely enthusiasm for what I was doing.

I would also like to thank a number of friends whose interest in this project and encouraging words helped me see it to completion. Thanks to Sarah Binder, Forrest Maltzman, Lisa Disch, Steven Gerencser, Kim Curtis, and Rom Coles. I would also like to thank my sisters—Pam, Karla, and Paula—for their interest in this project and their enthusiasm as it moved (slowly at times) from one stage to the next.

This book also benefitted from the timely arrival of Eva Catherine Clelland to our friends, Jennifer Clelland and Brian Nichols. Eva's birth in June 1998 was perfectly timed so that I could do some final interviews for the book in Minnesota, see her birth, and get back to North Carolina in time to finish my revisions and meet my July deadline.

In writing this book, I had a distinct advantage over most writers in that I am married to political theorist and book writer Susan Bickford. Susan's ability to process and distill an argument and help others to do the same is (not to put too fine a point on it) remarkable. The book benefitted immeasurably from her insightful comments, challenging questions, and careful editing, and I have benefitted immeasurably from her marvelous companionship throughout our years together.

Finally, it was at home with my parents where I became intrigued by politics, as my Dad and I would debate the latest issue of *Time* magazine. And it was there that I first came to appreciate the importance of learning. For these lessons and their many years of support, I thank my mother, Ruth McAvoy, and my father, the late Ken McAvoy.

*Controlling Technocracy:*
*Citizen Rationality and the Nimby Syndrome*

CHAPTER 1

# *Introduction*

Nimbys are noisy. Nimbys are powerful. Nimbys are everywhere. Nimbys are people who live near enough to corporate or government projects and are upset enough about them to work to stop, stall, or shrink them. Nimbys organize, march, sue, and petition to block the developers they think are threatening them. They twist the arms of politicians, and they learn how to influence regulators. They fight fiercely and then, win or lose, they vanish.[1]

The Nimby syndrome is a public health problem of the first order. It is a recurring mental illness which continues to infect the public. Organizations which intensify this illness are like the viruses and the bacteria which have, over the centuries, caused epidemics such as the plague.[2]

Reports of the failures of the American political system are common, but those who analyze political decision-making in the context of Nimby issues offer some of the strongest indictments. According to these critics, policymaking is corrupted by self-interested or irrational citizens who misuse the democratic process and lead policymakers away from optimal solutions to social problems. Implicitly (and at times explicitly), they argue that we would be collectively better off relying on bureaucratic decision-making guided by policy experts, rather than continuing to suffer under a democratic process that leaves us at the mercy of uninformed citizens. By characterizing the Nimby syndrome as a plague, these critics (e.g., Beckmann 1973; Ophuls 1977, 1992; Inhaber 1998) warn that this phenomenon is widespread, "infecting" a variety of issues, particularly technical decisions about the safe disposal of hazardous waste.

If the Nimby syndrome is a plague, it is not surprising that it is a modern one. Over the last fifty years we have witnessed a dramatic development in the state's administrative capacity and a commitment to use that capacity to solve social problems. At the same time, opportunities for citizens to express their policy preferences through elections, public hearings, open meeting laws, referenda, and public opinion polls have increased (Cronin 1989; Gormley 1989). These relatively incompatible trends, one toward centralization of policymaking and the other toward decentralization of procedures, strain existing democratic institutions. Inevitably, those unhappy with the policies chosen in the midst of these competing trends argue that the policymaking process is either too insulated or too open to influence.

This tension over the appropriate role for citizens and policy experts played itself out in Minnesota throughout the '80s and into the '90s, as the state used various strategies to site a hazardous waste facility. In 1990 residents of Red Lake County in northern Minnesota cast their ballots in a referendum on the state's proposed hazardous waste facility. The facility was resoundingly rejected by the residents, effectively ending Minnesota's decade-long search for a site. For state officials and other supporters of the facility, this case represented yet another manifestation of the Nimby syndrome, whereby local residents put their fears ahead of the general welfare and prevented the state from building a much needed facility. The facility was rejected despite considerable efforts on the part of the state to make the decision-making process voluntary and participatory. Opponents of the facility argued that it was incompatible with a rural economy, not necessary given the amount of waste generated in the state, and, if sited, belonged closer to the main source of production, Minneapolis/St. Paul.

At first blush, Minnesota's experience sounds all too familiar to those who study the Nimby syndrome—local communities refuse to accept a facility designed to serve the state's general economic and environmental welfare. However, as one digs deeper into Minnesota's experience, the Nimby explanation for the failure of the site faces important challenges. In this case study of Minnesota's unsuccessful attempt to site a hazardous waste stabilization and containment facility, I argue that this siting effort should not be seen as another failure due to irrational and self-interested citizens who subverted a well-conceived and essential disposal facility, nor as a failure in siting strategy. Through a detailed comparison of citizens and elite claims about the facility, I show that many of the sources of disagreement between citizens and siting officials involve value trade-offs rather than technical issues, and contend that state officials' views on these matters should not take precedence. More important, the comparison demonstrates that citizens who opposed the facility often had significant and quite sensible critiques of state officials' plans, given the nature of Minnesota's hazardous waste problems and the ways the state proposed to address them.

The Nimby syndrome gained prominence in the 1970s as concern arose among researchers and the popular press that citizens could routinely and most often successfully oppose facilities like those for hazardous waste disposal. The concern was that society as a whole would not receive the benefits from safe disposal of hazardous waste because no one was willing to bear the localized costs.

In its early and popular usage, the Nimby syndrome characterized citizens as (a) overly emotional, uninformed, and unscientific in their opposition to these facilities; (b) motivated by narrow, selfish interests; and (c) obstructing policies that would provide for the collective good. Recent studies of the Nimby syndrome challenge the first two of these characteristics. Researchers have attempted to understand the Nimby syndrome using survey data and to demonstrate that citizens are not entirely motivated by self-interest and narrow concerns. For example, in their study of West Virginia, Hunter and Leyden (1995) argue that citizens who oppose facilities because they are concerned about health issues or do not trust government officials have legitimate reservations and are not afflicted by the Nimby syndrome. In addition, researchers have begun to question whether experts' emphasis on the *probability* of an accident should take precedence over the value-laden assessments of citizens about the *consequences* of an accident (Kunreuther and Slovic 1996).

Also, researchers have examined whether the siting strategies used by public officials have heightened citizens' concerns and intensified their opposition. Those studying hazardous waste siting show that the failure of early siting attempts is not surprising given that officials often tried to impose facilities on local communities or relied on eminent domain (Rabe 1994). Thus, greater emphasis has been placed on communicating to citizens the risks associated with facilities (Leiss 1996) and finding fair siting procedures as a way to overcome citizen opposition (Gerrard 1994; Rabe 1994; Frey and Oberholzer-Gee 1996; Frey, Oberholzer-Gee, and Eichenberger 1996).[3]

Although these studies have provided valuable information about citizen motivations and the utility of different siting strategies, the recent Nimby literature can be read as a defense of democratic decision-making on the grounds that citizens are not wholly selfish and parochial and that their participation in the process will help them see the need for a facility. Gerrard (1994) argues that citizen participation is justified because of the need for fairness in siting decisions. These are important findings and claims, but they do not provide evidence that citizen participation is actually helpful and necessary to effective problem-solving, even when citizens oppose hazardous waste sites.[4] Importantly, the emphasis in the Nimby literature on effective siting strategies and citizen attitudes means most scholars have left state officials' claims about the need for and safety of facilities unchallenged for the most part.[5]

As this case shows, there are a variety of important questions for understanding the Nimby syndrome and the appropriate role for citizens in policymaking that arise when looking at the context in which public officials make siting decisions. What are state officials' motivations for siting facilities? How do they respond to public pressures? How do they use resources to influence the debate? Are the positions the state advances superior to those arrived at through citizen deliberation? What kind of control of bureaucratic decision-making is possible, necessary, or desirable? In this case, an examination of the political and institutional setting in which the siting decisions were made shows that state officials' decision-making was improved because they were repeatedly scrutinized by citizens concerned about the facility.

In studying the Nimby syndrome through Minnesota's siting experience, I am continually drawn to conceptualize the decision-making process as a struggle between technocracy and democracy.[6] Although in Minnesota the siting process evolved over time and was neither wholly technocratic nor democratic, this characterization provides an important lens through which to see the state's motivations for siting this facility, its response to citizen opposition, and its efforts to get the public to see the facility as safe and necessary. As state officials strategized about the facility, citizens were urging them to see the ways in which their perspective was flawed, and the citizens hoped to highlight the issues of fairness and equity that were central to the debate. It was this ongoing battle over control of the state's siting policy and the terms under which policy should be made that characterized Minnesota's siting effort.

In the remainder of this chapter, I summarize some key features of the Nimby debate when viewed from the context of the technocracy/democracy debate.

## *The Development of State Power and Support for Expert Decision-Making*

Tocqueville noted long ago that Americans are ambivalent about the role that citizens and government officials should play in decision-making.

> Our contemporaries are ever prey to two conflicting passions: They feel the need for guidance, and they long to stay free. Unable to wipe out these two contradictory instincts, they try to satisfy them both together. Their imagination conceives of government which is unitary, protective, and all powerful, but elected by the people. Centralization is combined with sovereignty of the people.[7]

As the scope of government and complexity of the issues facing it continue to grow, the tension between the need for guidance on policy matters and the desire to preserve citizen sovereignty is even more evident today. Issues like the disposal of hazardous waste challenge our commitment to democratic decision-making. Some, like those concerned about the Nimby syndrome, contend that we would be better off relying exclusively on policy experts and state officials to resolve difficult issues. Others fear that as we increasingly rely on the state's administrative capacity to guide us, we risk giving up democratic self-rule as "administrative governance" is transformed into "administrative despotism" (Tocqueville 1969, 642).

The history of hazardous waste siting in the United States and the evolution of the Nimby syndrome is replete with examples of technocratic thinking. Studies of the early efforts to site hazardous waste facilities show that both state and local governments adopted strategies that have been characterized as preemptive, regulatory, and managerial.[8] These strategies rely on the state's powers of eminent domain and professional expertise to site facilities. Such strategies are pursued by policymakers in the hope that they will lead to quick resolution of the issue and successful siting. As Rabe (1994) argues:

> Managerial or regulatory approaches thus depoliticize procedures such as siting by substituting expert judgment for public deliberation or

decision making by elected officials. They presume that no entity can rival state or provincial agencies for understanding waste management needs and establishing preferred site location. (45)

Those who endorse technocratic solutions to controversial political issues believe that policy experts, isolated from political pressures, can make decisions that will best serve the general welfare.

The potential benefit of greater reliance on state officials to decide policy issues is described in recent political science analyses of the state's administrative capacity as well as those examining hazardous waste policy. Among the state theorists, the state is often viewed as a benign force in politics—that is, the state can use its coercive powers and technical expertise to benefit the polity as as whole.[9] Rather than being held captive by those advancing particularistic claims, an autonomous state can overcome these narrow pressures and pursue its vision of the common good.

This view of the state as both a decision-maker and a problem-solver is most clearly expressed in the opening chapter of *Bringing the State Back In.* In showing the commonality between her statist argument and Hugh Heclo's, Skocpol argues:

Without being explicitly presented as such, Heclo's book is about autonomous state contributions to social policy making. But the autonomous state actions Heclo highlights are not all acts of coercion or domination; they are, instead, the intellectual activities of civil administrators engaging in diagnosing societal problems and framing policy alternatives to deal with them. (1985, 11)[10]

Although Skocpol concedes that the state can act narrowly, self-interestedly, and perhaps stupidly, she goes on to argue that "we need not entirely dismiss the possibility that partially or fully autonomous state actions *may* be able to address problems and even find 'solutions' beyond the reach of societal actors and those parts of government closely constrained by them" (1985, 15). She thus embraces a vision of good policy as that which is made above the fray of partisan politics and in the more "rational" setting of an insulated bureaucracy.[11]

In *Defending the National Interest,* Krasner makes an even stronger claim that the general welfare emerges out of isolated and independent decisionmaking rather than intensely partisan policymaking. Drawing on the work of Vilfredo Pareto, he argues, "Utility *for* the community involves summing the preferences of individual members of a community. The utility *of* the community involves making judgments about the well-being of the community as a whole" (1978, 12). Therefore the general welfare is not found in the preferences of individual citizens, but is discovered by political leaders who can "objectively" understand what is the best interest *of* a community.[12] For Krasner, state decision-makers understand and pursue the general welfare. "State objectives refer in this study to utility *of* the community and will be called the nation's general or national interest" (1978, 6).

This benign view of the state and elite decision-making finds its way into studies of environmental policy and risk management as well. In his study *Breaking the Vicious Circle,* Stephen Breyer (1993) argues that citizens routinely over-estimate the risks of potential environmental threats like hazardous waste and asbestos and urge public officials to propose remedies that are too costly for the potential benefit. Breyer proposes a relatively insulated board, similar to the Office of Management and Budget, that would oversee risk management policies and ensure that they are feasible and cost-effective.

In a similar vein, many discussions of hazardous waste policy implicitly assume that the experts' preferred solution—siting—is essential to the management of hazardous waste (e.g., Morell 1984; Mazmanian and Morell 1990. (For a critique, see Gerrard 1994.) Therefore evaluations of siting efforts often fail to question whether the attempts themselves are necessary. Often it is assumed that the state is pursuing the general welfare while trying to accommodate the self-interested claims of citizens near the proposed facility. Observers frequently do not take seriously the claims by citizens that a proposed site might be redundant with existing facilities, unnecessary given the amount of waste generated in the area, unsafe due to geological or land-use characteristics, or a disincentive to recycling and reclamation.[13]

## The Problem of Political Control

Max Weber, one of the earliest and most insightful critics of bureaucracy, understood the promise that bureaucracy held for modern democratic societies, yet he despaired over the threat that a highly structured bureaucracy posed for democratic governance. In his writing on bureaucracy, Weber stresses two aspects of the state's administrative capacity. First, he extols the virtues of an administrative state which can lend expertise, impartiality, and uniformity to the implementation of public policy. The administrative state can provide fair and effective *means* to democratically decided *ends*. But Weber is also sensitive to the tension between bureaucratization and democracy and to how this tension might be resolved at the expense of democratic decision-making. Modern democracies must rely on bureaucracies to administer decisions made through democratic institutions, yet "[w]e must remember this fact . . . that 'democracy' as such is opposed to the 'rule of bureaucracy', in spite and perhaps because of its unavoidable yet unintended promotion of bureaucratization" (Weber 1946, 47).

However, through their development of professional skills, technical expertise, and decision-making authority, bureaucrats often emerge as the principal actor in policymaking.

> Under normal conditions, the power position of a fully developed bureaucracy is always overtowering. The "political master" finds himself in the position of the "dilettante" who stands opposite the "expert", facing the trained official who stands within the management of administration. (Weber 1946, 47)[14]

In other words, state actors move beyond their "ideal" role of deciding on the means and begin to influence the ends of policymaking as well. As state administrators develop greater expertise in their policy area and insulated organizational structures, political control of policymaking becomes remote.

The recent writings of Robert Dahl and Charles Lindblom take this critique by Weber further and reveal the more pernicious side of technocratic decision-making and autonomous state actions. Both writers, to varying degrees, stress the interrelated nature of moral and instrumental knowledge in making public policy and the inherent practical and normative problems that stem from technocratic decision-making.

In his critique of technocratic decision-making, Dahl stresses the connection between the moral and instrumental components of policymaking and that it is precisely because of this interconnectedness that technocratic decision-making is incapable of producing policies for the common good. Summarizing the argument of advocates of technocratic decision-making, Dahl says:

Instrumental knowledge, the argument might continue, is primarily, perhaps exclusively, *empirical* knowledge about mankind, society, nature, human and social behavior, tendencies, laws, processes, structures, and the like. In principle, then, the instrumental knowledge necessary to govern well could be a science like other empirical sciences. (1989, 67)

For example, on issues like nuclear weapons strategy, of central importance is the instrumental knowledge of where targets are, what constitutes an effective deterrence, and the capability of enemies to launch a first strike. However, Dahl argues that even the rarified circles of nuclear weapons strategy are infused with moral decisions. For instance, the targeting of cities and other population centers as part of a nuclear strategy is more than a strategic decision, it is a deeply moral one.

Likewise, on hazardous waste policymaking, value judgments are interwoven with technical arguments. Decisions to site hazardous waste facilities in a community impose risks on those living near the facility or along the transportation routes while providing the benefits of safe disposal and a clean environment to those not in contact with the facility. Who should benefit and who should pay the costs or be at risk are important value judgments which are made in the decision-making process, whether those issues are explicitly raised or not.[15]

Lindblom (1990) makes a similar claim in arguing that technocrats often come to an understanding of the "common good" and defend it as though it were objectively arrived at and neutral. However, Lindblom contends their claims regarding the common good are better viewed as "common-good partisanship"—that is, they hold one vision of the common good, but it is partisan and should not be given higher standing than citizens' visions of the common good. Different claims by citizens and experts should be the starting point of deliberation over policymaking rather than excluding one group or the other from the debate.

Dahl and Lindblom push this critique further by questioning whether policy experts really have the technical understandings that they claim. "[P]recisely, because the knowledge of the policy elites is specialized, their expert knowledge ordinarily provides too narrow a base for the instrumental judgments that an intelligent policy would require" (Dahl 1989, 337).[16] Likewise, Lindblom (1965, Chapter 9) proposes that technocratic, or what he refers to as "synoptic decision-making," attempts to solve a problem by comprehensively understanding it, setting goals, weighing options, and pursuing a "rational" path toward those goals. Unfortunately, Lindblom argues, modern political problems are difficult to comprehend fully because of humans' limited intellectual capacity, inadequate information, and the costliness of an exhaustive search of policy alternatives. Therefore this technocratic ideal is likely to fail because it is not adapted to the openness and unpredictability of the social and physical environment.

Technocratic, or synoptic, decision-making strategies are commonly employed in siting decisions and often produce the results that Lindblom and Dahl predict. In the construction of a low-level nuclear waste site in New Mexico, vaults for storing nuclear waste were built into salt veins, which are structures generally free of water and stable. However, preliminary tests showed that experts were mistaken in their calculations about the speed at which the salt walls would encapsulate the waste cannisters and the movement of the cannisters once this occurred (Carter 1987).

Similarly, the Department of Energy chose Yucca Mountain, Nevada, as the disposal site for the nation's high-level nuclear waste because of the arid conditions and lack of human habitation. However, the adequacy of this site was first challenged in 1990 by a Department of Energy geologist who contended that this area experiences periodic flooding from underground aquifers that would thus make the site unsuitable for long-term storage (Broad 1990). This claim was studied by a seventeen-member panel and subsequently dismissed as a problem. Yet the Department of Energy is now investigating how to deal with the prospect of "a growing plume of ground water contaminated by radiation . . . from the Yucca Mountain repository site" (Carter and Pigford 1998). This plume could develop as water dripping from the ceiling of the containment tunnels causes the waste canisters to deteriorate and the radioactive run-off to make its way into underground aquifers. The aquifers would then carry the contaminated water supply to nearby inhabited areas. Although it is hoped that engineers can address this problem in their designs, this development further underscores the complexity of this disposal plan and raises questions about the ability of experts to safely manage nuclear waste.

The point that Dahl, in particular, stresses is not just that technocrats will make mistakes, but that because of the insulated nature of technical decision-making mistakes will go undetected. This is an important issue to raise in the context of hazardous waste siting since one of the ways in which sites are chosen is by relying on a board to decide whether a site is necessary and where it should be located. Often, once a site is selected states invoke their right to eminent domain. However, critics of technocratic decision-making would argue that the whole process should be open—from the decision about whether a site is needed, to where it should go, to the conditions through which it will be sited. Thus those suspicious of the technical superiority of policy experts see citizen opposition like that commonly associated with the Nimby syndrome as a necessary check on expert power and an important component of effective policymaking.

## Overview of the Case and Argument

The selection of a case with which to examine these issues of technical expertise and citizen participation will obviously influence the initial impressions that one can draw. A good case for understanding how citizens influence policymaking must confront citizens with a formidable adversary in the form of an activist, respected state with strong allies on an issue of high complexity. I must confess that, like Dahl's selection of New Haven, I chose Minnesota "for the most part because it lay conveniently at hand" (Dahl 1961, 5). However, the selection of both Minnesota as a case and hazardous waste policy as an issue area combine to make this a critical case through which to examine these issues of state autonomy, political control, and the role of citizens in the policymaking process.

Minnesota's state government has a reputation as activist, progressive, and directed toward problem-solving. This is consistent with Daniel Elazar's (1984) characterization of the state's political culture as moralistic. According to Elazar, states with moralistic political cultures like Minnesota are distinctive because their citizens view themselves as part of a community in which collective action (government-sponsored or privately initiated) can solve problems and social and economic regulation is seen as legitimate. In such political cultures, government will "initiate new programs without public pressure if [they are] believed to be in the public interest, and the bureaucracy is viewed positively" (Elazar 1984, 120–121). Because Minnesota's state government has a reputation for constructive problem-solving, it is likely to develop plans that citizens will consider legitimate and it should not encounter widespread public opposition to its initiatives. States with "individualistic" or "traditionalistic" political cultures tend to hold negative views of social and economic regulation since they see them as an unwelcome intrusion into the market (individualistic) or into the personal relationships that political elites establish with their supporters (traditionalistic).

Looking at several measures of the scope of the government in Minnesota, it is clear that it ranks high relative to other states. For example, Minnesota is comparable to other states in the ratio of private- to public-sector employment (it is 15 percent in Minnesota, and this is close to the national average [Hovey and Hovey 1998]). However, in comparison to other states, Minnesota appears to have a greater capacity to extract resources. For instance, Minnesota ranks fifth in the nation in general revenue raised per capita. And state employees, in part, appear to be beneficiaries of this revenue-generating capacity, since they rank seventh in the nation in earnings (U.S. Statistical Abstract 1990). These general patterns of an activist state in Minnesota translate into commitment of resources and promulgation of regulations in protecting the environment. Minnesota is ranked seventh best among the fifty states in the Green Policy Initiatives rating, which evaluates states on their ability to adopt innovative policies on a broad range of environmental issues. The state also ranks fifth on the Green Index, which provides a comprehensive assessment of the state's environmental health, policies, and political leadership on environmental issues.[17]

In addition, Minnesota has clearly made hazardous waste siting a priority since the later 1970s, when it received an EPA grant to site a disposal facility in the state. The state government received strong support early in the process from influential groups like 3M and other waste producers, as well as from notable environmental groups. Most important, Minnesota policymakers made a strong commitment to siting a facility and devoted $10 million to the siting effort from 1980 to 1989.

These factors combine to make Minnesota an important and severe test case for examining how citizens can challenge state decision-makers and for assessing the consequences for policymaking. Given the state of Minnesota's history as a problem-solver, its available resources, and its obvious commitment to and expertise in environmental policymaking, it is less likely that citizens will be able to develop convincing critiques of Minnesota's policies than in a state with little expertise or a poor track record in these matters.

Included in this case study is an examination of citizen opinion in two rural counties that were candidates for the state's stabilization and containment facility for hazardous waste—Red Lake County and Koochiching County (see Fig. 1.1). Both counties are important to study because citizens in each had numerous interactions with policymakers. County officials and

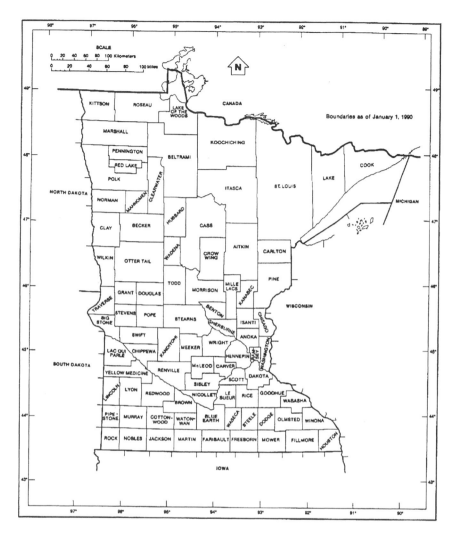

*Figure 1.1* Counties of Minnesota
Source: *U.S. Department of Commerce, Economics and Statistics Administration, Bureau of the Census.*

the Minnesota Waste Management Board held a number of informational meetings and public hearings to inform citizens about the proposed site and the risks involved, as well as to get their feedback. Because of their extensive involvement in the issue, these counties can provide significant information about how citizens viewed the problem of hazardous waste, how they evaluated the proposed solutions, and how they attempted to influence policy-making. Given the fact that these are rural counties and are likely to have a smaller, less technically sophisticated population than urban counties, this case provides an even stricter test of the claim that citizens can provide in-depth and cogent critiques of the state's siting efforts and gain access to decision-making.

Moreover, because of the technical components of hazardous waste policymaking, this case provides an important example from which to examine the tension between the need for guidance and the risks it presents to citizen sovereignty. Disposal of hazardous wastes requires some scientific understanding of the dangers that certain chemicals pose to the environment and people's health. However, because the issue is complex and its effects are far-reaching, hazardous waste policy requires a number of value judgments which are not generally amenable to the "scientific" tools policy experts use to guide the process, and which are more appropriately made by citizens. Decisions about the siting of hazardous waste facilities involve issues of fairness: who bears the risk of a leak in the disposal system, who benefits as a result of a clean environment, and how safe the system must be to protect future generations from risk.[18] This study will highlight the differences between citizens and experts in making normative judgments about policy decisions and the questions that these differences raise in terms of society's reliance on expert decision-making.

My analysis of Minnesota's hazardous waste policy falls into two related parts. In the first part I examine the various actors in the policymaking process and the extent to which the state's technical experts are controlled by factors inside or outside of existing political institutions (e.g., legislators, interest groups, etc.). In addition, I consider the role of citizens in providing a check on the state's claims of expertise. My case study approach allows me to examine in detail the obstacles citizens face in gaining access to the policy process and the extent to which these obstacles can be overcome.

The second part of this analysis focuses on the consequences of citizen involvement in policy issues like the siting of hazardous waste facilities. To this end, I will compare the claims of the Minnesota Waste Management Board.[19] to those of citizens in the counties that were potential hosts of a hazardous waste disposal facility. This will allow me to contrast the citizens' views of hazardous waste and notions of the "common good" to those of state officials and to assess whether a democratic solution, wherein citizens influence policy, is more effective than a technocratic one.

I begin Chapter 2 by describing Minnesota's decision-making process to demonstrate the importance of policy elites—legislators, interest groups, and state administrators in the Waste Management Board—in structuring public policy. This includes an examination of the relationship between the Waste Management Board and the Legislative Commission on Waste Management (LCWM). Members of the legislature gave the Legislative Commission on Waste Management considerable discretion in its dealings with the Waste Management Board, and the LCWM in turn gave the Waste Management Board a lot of latitude in its decision-making. This analysis will demonstrate the development of a policy network between influential interest groups and state administrators and the role that these negotiations had in policy formation. However, this elite bargaining between state officials and important interest groups was eventually disrupted as the result of mobilized citizen opposition to the proposed policy.

Chapter 3 outlines the negotiations between the state and citizens in the counties and reveals the strategies that the state used in trying to gain citizen cooperation. Most important, it demonstrates how the state can use its noncoercive powers like financial and human resources to enhance its capacity to make decisions. In this case, the state's strategy was to shift the issue from hazardous waste to economic development. It used a voluntary siting process in which members of county boards could volunteer their counties as potential sites for the facility. This helped the state by giving it support from respected officials in the community. Waste Management Board officials engaged in an extensive public relations campaign to persuade citizens that the facility was safe and in their best interest. They monitored the local media and provided information about their activities to those newspapers and television stations which were generally supportive of the project. Examining these negotiations confirms that citizens have little influence on the shape and structure of policy, but despite the state's best efforts, they can have some success curtailing its capacity by vetoing its policy proposals.

Chapter 4 shows the differences between citizens and state actors regarding Minnesota's hazardous waste problem and the proposed solutions. In addition, it reveals state officials' deep skepticism of citizen opposition to their hazardous waste proposal. These differences are evident from the debate between the citizens in two rural counties and Minnesota's Waste Management Board. Survey data, interviews, and newspaper accounts help clarify the commonalities and differences between citizens and policymakers. First, I provide some background information about the two counties that had extensive experience with this issue, elaborating on their motivations for involvement and the nature of public opinion within the county. Second, I highlight the differences in perceptions between citizens and state officials about risks and benefits associated with the facility. Third, I compare citizens' and state officials' opinions over some policy alternatives. Fourth, by using survey data, I test whether the variety of factors found in interviews and newspapers are equally influential in citizens' thinking or if some weigh more heavily than others. This analysis includes a covariance structure model, estimated with LISREL (Linear Structural Relations) as a way of assessing the relative importance of the variety of factors thought to influence citizens' attitudes toward the facility. Included are measures of perceived risk of the facility, need for the facility, attitudes toward an urban versus a rural location, and trust in government on both technical issues like hazardous waste and other issues like taxes, welfare, and agricultural policy.[20] In the end, this chapter reveals that citizens can provide formidable critiques of state initiatives, and it demonstrates the fallibility of policy experts in forming a solution to the hazardous waste problem.

In Chapter 5 I stress the ways in which citizen opposition to the state's proposals actually improved policymaking rather than detracting from it. I make this claim based on an analysis of the evolution of the state's hazardous waste policy after the siting effort failed. The state's commitment in the 1990s to recycling, reclamation, and reduction and the benefits produced by these policies cast doubt on the state's claims in the 1980s that it needed the facility. In addition, the adoption and success of these policies showed the prescience of citizens when they urged the state to reduce the waste stream prior to a large investment in a disposal facility. In this final chapter I also discuss the ways in which the findings from this study suggest alternative strategies for making hazardous waste policy.

## Notes

1. William Glaberson, "Coping in the Age of 'Nimby,' " *New York Times,* 19 June 1988, sec. 3, 1.

2. Report from the Southern California Waste Forum. The Southern California Waste Forum was a meeting of government officials and business representatives to discuss California's waste problems. (Quote is from Piller 1991, 4.)

3. Siting strategies have been studied extensively. The most thorough accounts of these strategies can be found in Mazmanian and Morell (1992) and Munton (1996). Earlier studies of siting are Morell and Magorian (1982); Andrews (1988); Davis and Lester (1988); and Mazmanian and Morell (1990).

4. There are some exceptions to this general reluctance to acknowledge the constructive role that citizens can play in hazardous waste policy. For example, Matheny and Williams (1988) stress the importance of democratic procedures in hazardous waste siting for citizens to gain knowledge and be able to meaningfully participate. Also, in his study of Alberta, Rabe (1994) shows that citizens helped to structure the policies that would guide the province's waste management.

In their study of radioactive waste disposal, Kraft and Clary (1991) examine this issue of citizen rationality in policymaking directly and find that citizens are not simply myopic and irrational in making policy decisions and that citizen challenges to radioactive waste disposal contribute to effective policymaking.

5. For exceptions see Williams and Matheny (1995) and Rabe (1994). In his discussion of Alberta, Rabe argues for the importance of a check on the policy proposals of state officials and suggests that citizens can contribute to policymaking by challenging their proposals. Also, Lake (1993) directly challenges claims that these disposal facilities are necessary and argues that they are being sited for the benefit of businesses, not the general welfare.

6. Williams and Matheny (1995) identify different models of policymaking for hazardous waste. What I call the technocratic model is similar to their managerial model. The managerial model puts policy experts at the center of decision-making and suggests that their preferences should be given priority in policymaking. What I refer to as the democratic model is similar to their dialogic model, in which a variety of perspectives are part of the policymaking process and decisions are arrived at through deliberation rather than through proclamation.

7. Alexis de Tocqueville, *Democracy in America* (Garden City, NY: Doubleday, 1969).

8. Although the strategies outlined here were more common in the early hazardous waste siting attempts, states like Arizona, Florida, Georgia, New Jersey, and New York were using them as recently as 1992 (Rabe 1994, 46).

9. There is an important debate about the novelty and usefulness of "state theories." For sampling, see Almond, (1988) Nordlinger, (1988) and Lowi (1988) in the *American Political Science Review*. Rather than address the overall merits of this research program here, I simply use some of these state theorists to demonstrate how state actors can justify their willingness to ignore societal pressures.

10. Heclo himself says:

Governments not only "power" (or whatever the verb form of that approach might be); they also puzzle. Policy-making is a form of collective puzzlement on society's behalf; it entails both deciding and knowing. The process of making pension, unemployment and superannuation policies has extended beyond deciding what "wants" to accommodate, to include problems of knowing who might want something, what is wanted, what should be wanted, and how to turn even the most sweet-tempered general agreement into a concrete collective action. This process is political, not because all policy is a by-product of power and conflict but because some men have undertaken to act in the name of others. (1974, 305; as quoted in Skocpol 1985, 11)

11. Skocpol (1985) argues that she is neutral on this question of whether state autonomy and capacity are "good" for society. However, her research clearly highlights the problem-solving capacity of the state while giving little attention to the consequences that this has for democratic governance.

12. Robert Dahl (1989) describes these two approaches to understanding interests as "organismic" (utility *of* the community) and "humanistic" (utility *for* the community).

13. See Kraft and Clary (1991) for an argument which does take seriously the role that citizens can play in making siting decisions. Gerrard (1994) takes issue with the idea that siting is the only viable way to address the hazardous waste problem. He notes that the high price of disposal has encouraged waste reduction.

14. In this essay Weber is arguing that legislators, rather than the general public, serve as a "political master" over the bureaucracy.

15. For an argument about the ways in which values enter into assessments of risk, see Kunreuther and Slovic (1996). Here they take issue with the idea that risk can be objectively assessed. As an example, they cite research which shows that

Between 1950 and 1970 coal mines became much less risky in terms of deaths from accidents per ton of coal, but they became marginally riskier in terms of deaths from accidents per worker. From a national point of view, given that a certain amount of coal has to be obtained, deaths per million tons of coal is the more appropriate measure of risk, whereas from a labor leader's point of view, deaths per thousand miners employed may be more relevant. (119–120)

16. Similarly, Lindblom's *Inquiry and Change* is devoted to the notion that social science knowledge, both in academic and policymaking settings, is deeply impaired and should have a circumscribed role in policy. Social scientists and political elites suffer from an impaired understanding of social problems because they try to silence dissent, have a tendency toward convergent thinking, and maintain a benign view of the role of government, to name a few of the causes.

17. These rankings from the Green Index are from Bob Hall and Mary Lee, *1991–1992 Green Index: A State-By-State Guide to the Environmental Health* (Washington, D.C.: Island Press, 1991, 148), and reported in Lester (1994, 56–57). Lester (1994) combines the Green Index with a measure of the state's institutional capacity in general. With this system, Minnesota is categorized as a struggler (i.e., a state with a commitment to the environment but with limited institutional capacity to implement its policies). However, since the Green Index and the Green Policy Initiative include indicators of environ-

mental policies that states have implemented, these seem like more valid measures of states' performance in this area.

18. For a detailed discussion of fairness and risk in siting decisions, see Gerrard 1994. For a recent empirical assessment of the role of fair procedures in citizens' willingness to accept a facility, see Frey and Oberholzer-Gee (1996).

19. In 1989 the Waste Management Board was reorganized and named the Office of Waste Management. In 1994 the legislature restructured the agency again and renamed it the Office of Environmental Assistance (OEA). However, for consistency's sake and to avoid confusion, I will refer to it by its original name.

20. By technical issues I mean those in which scientific knowledge plays a role in decision-making. Clearly, issues like tax policy are quite complex but do not require the same type of technical background to understand as the issue of a nuclear or hazardous waste disposal facility.

# CHAPTER 2

# Elite Policy Networks and Political Control in Policymaking

Bureaucracy is *the* means of carrying "community action" over into rationally ordered "social action." Therefore, as an instrument for "societalizing" relations of power, bureaucracy has been and is a power instrument of the first order—for the one who controls the bureaucratic apparatus.

Max Weber
"Essay on Bureaucracy"

As noted at the beginning of Chapter 1, the Nimby syndrome has on more than one occasion been characterized as a plague—a plague of overly emotional and parochial citizens who oppose state-led initiatives and undermine the general welfare. This view implies that citizens are able to wrestle control of policymaking from state officials, business representatives, and environmental groups supportive of siting and that the technocratic ideal of rational and objective decision-making is rarely met. However, decision-making about Minnesota's hazardous waste policy reveals something other than overt control by citizens of the policymaking process and powerless state officials. In this chapter I look at the struggle for control of policymaking by businesses, influential interest groups, legislators, state officials, and citizens. I argue that citizens had limited influence over the general direction of the state's policy, whereas state officials were able to exercise considerable control. In the second stage of the siting process in particular, state officials developed the autonomy to design a policy that they felt was in the state's best interest.

## Theoretical Framework for Examining Hazardous Waste Policy

In this section I describe the analytical tools and key concepts that guide this study of Minnesota's hazardous waste policy. I begin by examining the issue of political control and the role that citizens can play in this process. In turn, I focus on state theorists' distinction between state autonomy and state capacity, and show how this is useful for understanding the contours of state officials' control of policymaking.

The extent to which the administrative state is held in check by democratic institutions has long been a source of concern for students of American politics.[1] Mid-twentieth-century political scientists provided a defense of the American political system, arguing that the mix of representative democracy with periodic elections and the rise of interest group politics provided sufficient check on the exercise of political power by the state (Dahl 1961; Truman 1951). In the 1960s and 1970s the effectiveness of this form of democratic control of the bureaucracy was questioned as the oligopolistic tendencies of interest group politics were exposed. Theodore Lowi (1979), in particular, spearheaded this indictment of interest group politics, contending that the broad delegation of authority granted to state administrators resulted in the "capture" of public authority by specialized, private interests. Democratic control of the bureaucracy fails, in his opinion, because legislators avoid making the difficult political decisions required for effective and accountable policymaking and state administrators are left to bargain and negotiate with elite interest groups to make policy decisions.

Alternatively, Charles Lindblom (1977, 1982) traces the lack of democratic control of policymaking to the market system rather than to the political system. He contends that modern policymaking is biased toward the preferences of privileged groups—namely, business interests. These business interests use their market power to coerce state decision-makers to ensure that their policy preferences are met. The policymaking process thus lacks democratic accountability because the market system bestows decision-making authority regarding the allocation of resources on private actors who can in turn use control over resources to gain favorable rulings from state administrators.

The argument that democratic institutions are not in control of policymaking is also made by Neo-Weberians, such as Skocpol and Stephen Krasner, who find that state actors often form "policy networks" with elite interest groups and conduct ongoing negotiations with these groups to make policy.[2] However, the Neo-Weberians also argue that the organizational structure of the state can at times enable public officials to act independently. Specifically, when state officials possess specialized skills and maintain hierarchical control over decision-making, they can often pursue their own policy objectives, even in the face of strong objections from influential groups. For state theorists, understanding policymaking requires an examination of the strength of organized groups and their patterned relations with state actors, as well as the capacity of state actors to resist these pressures.

Despite different understandings of how policy is made, these three perspectives arrive at the same conclusion—policymaking in the context of the modern administrative state is not subject to democratic control. This conclusion is drawn primarily because state actors are given broad grants of authority to make policy and often must negotiate their decisions with influential organized groups. Political control of the policymaking process by the legislative or executive branches is missing or ineffective.

This conclusion is challenged by Matthew McCubbins and Thomas Schwartz, who offer an innovative look at legislative oversight of administrative decision-making by distinguishing between *kinds* of political control.[3] McCubbins and Schwartz (1984) argue that control of the bureaucracy can take two forms—centralized and decentralized. Centralized control requires that legislators continually monitor administrative activities to ensure that state administrators are held accountable. They characterize this as the "police-patrol" model and argue that it is consistent with the conventional view of how political control of the bureaucracy should be conducted. However, they juxtapose this characterization of oversight and control with a decentralized approach, in which legislators address problems of bureaucratic performance when they arise and are brought to their attention rather than continually seeking them out. Therefore problems will be brought to the attention of legislators by constituents who are disappointed with or hostile to the decisions made by state administrators. These groups or citizens will then pressure their representatives to redirect administrative decision-making to coincide with their preferences (the "fire-alarm" model).[4]

Rather than seeing the decentralized and reactive approach as an abdication of responsibility and signaling a defect in the political system, McCubbins and Schwartz view this approach as a sensible, rational solution for holding a large bureaucracy in check. A number of studies on political control of bureaucracy argue that the influence of political institutions is quite evident when looking at the outputs of bureaucrats' regulatory activities (e.g., inspections of facilities, regulatory violations, etc.; see Wood 1988, Wood and Waterman 1991, Krause 1996).[5]

This idea of *decentralized* and *reactive* political control has important implications for understanding the role that citizens can play in the policy process. This model of political control can only work when legislators listen to and take seriously the claims that citizens make about effective policymaking. Legislators are dependent on citizens—who are perhaps focused on narrow issues, perhaps emotionally charged—to alert them to problems. Alternatively, if citizens were silenced in the way that those concerned about the Nimby syndrome would prefer, a vital check on state administrators and their plans to implement policies would be lost.

Although McCubbins and Schwartz demonstrate the importance of distinguishing between kinds of political control (centralized vs. decentralized), state theorists develop two important concepts—state autonomy and state capacity—which are helpful in identifying the type of control that *citizens* can exert. These theorists help us understand whether citizens limit the autonomy of state officials to develop public policies or they curtail officials' capacity to implement them.

According to state theorists, state officials act autonomously when their decision-making is motivated by institutional pressures and personal commitments and not by societal forces like mobilized citizens or elite interest groups. Here, autonomy refers to the development of interests and policy preferences by state officials. In her work Skocpol emphasizes the organizational features of the state as instrumental in the development of autonomous state actors. She argues that bureaucratic experience and administrative structures help state officials narrow policy choices and determine what is an acceptable strategy for problem-solving.[6] Similarly, Krasner explains the evolution of autonomous preferences by showing how state officials develop ideological commitments to the general welfare. Individuals working in insulated bureaucratic settings become socialized to the norms, rules, and culture that govern behavior and decision-making in an agency. Krasner shows how agencies dealing with international economic issues develop an agencywide commitment to the "national interest," which informs their policy preferences and leads them to resist pressures from important economic actors.[7]

In addition to investigating autonomy, state theorists examine the *capacity* of state actors to pursue their policy objectives (i.e., the power they have to successfully realize their interests). Like state autonomy, the capacity of the state is shaped by the institutional structure in which state actors are embedded. First, state capacity is often attenuated when the institutional structure of the state's administrative apparatus is decentralized or insulated, or when influential interest groups must be accommodated. Also, the reputation of agencies for competent administration and decision-making may influence the capacity that they have to pursue their own objectives (Downs 1967). Similarly, privileged access to information and strategic use of it can give state actors the opportunity to act independently. Finally, the scientific and legal issues surrounding a particular policy will influence the latitude that state actors have in decision-making (Weber 1946; Nordlinger 1981; Beetham 1987). For example, Woolley (1984) suggests that the complexity of monetary policy provides the Federal Reserve Board with a degree of independence from external pressures.

In the remainder of this chapter I use the theoretical frameworks described above to understand the relative influence of citizens and state officials in hazardous waste policy. This analysis begins with the state of Minnesota's initial attempt to site a hazardous waste disposal facility through an EPA grant. This failed siting attempt was instrumental in developing interest on the part of environmental groups, business groups, and state officials in hazardous waste policy. These groups worked together to develop the bill which would become the cornerstone of Minnesota's hazardous waste policy—the 1980 Waste Management Act. The cooperation between these groups continued into the implementation stage of the policy process as they ironed out differences and worked to overcome citizen opposition. However, citizens were able to insert themselves into the policy process through appeals to their legislators (as Schwartz and McCubbins suggest). But the extent of their involvement was limited to providing a check on the state's capacity to pursue the policies negotiated with elite interest groups, not to helping structure and design the policies that the state pursued. In other words, citizen involvement did not curb state autonomy.

Finally, this chapter will help specify the conditions under which the state can develop greater autonomy on issues like hazardous waste policy and the extent to which it can pursue its own course of action.

## Hazardous Waste Politics in Minnesota

Minnesota's first foray into hazardous waste disposal occurred in 1975 and was prompted by an EPA grant program to site hazardous waste facilities in urban areas. Minnesota officials were concerned about new restrictions on the disposal of certain chemicals in the sewer system. At the same time, EPA officials created this grant program to better understand the siting process, site development, and site operation, "including technical procedures, economics and other impacts."[8] The information gathered in this pilot project would serve as the foundation for the development of other hazardous waste projects as outlined in the Resource Conservation and Recovery Act (RCRA). Because the EPA had specific goals in mind,

> [c]ertain constraints were put on the project. These included that the site should be a chemical waste landfill, that it be in a metropolitan area, and that it would require technical upgrading to meet standards [i.e., that the site not necessarily be geologically ideal].[9]

The Minnesota Pollution Control Agency (MPCA) was awarded one of these EPA grants to find a site in the Minneapolis-St. Paul metro area, but because MPCA is a regulatory agency, it subcontracted the siting process to the Metropolitan Waste Control Commission (MWCC), a regulatory board governing waste disposal in the Twin Cities metropolitan area. The interest of MWCC in siting this facility arose from new ordinances that prohibited the disposal of industrial waste in the sewers without pretreatment. Waste that could not be pretreated would be placed in the new landfill, once sited.

The project was mired in controversy from the very beginning. The Metropolitan Waste Control Commission and the Minnesota Pollution Control Agency began the process by narrowing the list of possible sites in the metro area to four. Once the four finalists were selected, MWCC officials planned to publicize the project and allow for public input. Before the finalists were selected, however, metro area residents and politicians were informed of the project for the first time through reports in local newspapers:

Local reaction to the project and the process was uniformly negative. . . . Local residents and officials were outraged that they had not been contacted prior to the release of this information to the press and that such a dangerous facility should be located in their vicinity.[10]

This initial strategic mistake haunted the MWCC for the duration of the siting process. Public opinion remained strongly opposed to the facility, even after the MWCC had a chance to publicize its motivation for getting involved in this siting project. Local businesses were reluctant to publicly support the facility because of the bad publicity it had already received. In addition, without the support of local businesses and residents, elected politicians in the candidate areas were not willing to endorse the facility. By 1978 both the EPA and the MPCA recognized that the siting attempt was going to fail, and the grant was terminated.

The failure to site an urban landfill for hazardous waste disposal sensitized state legislators to the problem and provided the impetus for the state's next plan to manage Minnesota's hazardous waste by siting a facility. In the EPA's summary of the lessons of the siting project, it reported that "a new, long-term effort to site a hazardous waste management facility is currently underway in Minnesota. In many ways, this attempt reflects what the agencies involved in the previous effort feel are the lessons to be learned from the experience."[11]

## The Waste Management Act

In 1978 legislators formed the Joint Committee on Solid and Hazardous Waste to study waste issues in the state and to develop a new siting process which would provide Minnesota with a hazardous waste disposal facility. The failure of the EPA siting attempt served as an important lesson for decision-makers and interest groups associated with hazardous waste issues in the state. As a result of this failed siting attempt, key legislators were more cognizant of issues relating to the disposal of hazardous waste. They recognized that a thorough investigation into the scope of hazardous waste problems in Minnesota was necessary and that solutions to these problems should be found. At the same time, business groups within the state, particularly 3M, actively pressured the state to address Minnesota's hazardous waste problem.[12] Environmental groups also took an active interest in hazardous waste issues and worked to help shape the direction that the state would take in managing its hazardous waste problems. In Minnesota, the confluence of business, environmental, and state concerns provided the motivation to design and implement a new hazardous waste policy that could meet the goals of these three interests.

Through their study of the waste problem, legislators on the Joint Committee on Solid and Hazardous Waste found "that a large share of [hazardous waste] was not going into places that were designed to handle it; sanitary landfills, sewer systems. We didn't even have a very good idea of how much there was."[13] At the same time, Minnesota state legislators were worried about the threat that recent trends in hazardous waste policy and disposal capacity might pose for Minnesota businesses. Legislators working on the initial legislation expressed concerns that Minnesota businesses would be left without disposal capacity if stricter federal regulations caused some existing landfills to close. These legislators felt that the state needed to protect Minnesota's industrial production from potential disruption due to the unavailability of disposal facilities.[14] As a result of these concerns, legislators began writing the Waste Management Act, legislation that would allow the state to examine the nature of the problem and address the issue of disposal capacity.

During this study period businesses actively lobbied legislators to locate a hazardous waste landfill in the state because of their fears about the future availability of disposal sites in other states. Representatives from the 3M Corporation were particularly active in the formative stages of the legislation intended to address Minnesota's hazardous waste problems. Specifically, 3M's concern about disposal arose from the reclassification of the ash from its hazardous waste incinerator in Cottage Grove, Minnesota—a Twin Cities suburb:

About 1978 the Pollution Control Agency came up with the proposed standards for hazardous waste. Prior to that there were no standards defining what was hazardous waste. And in those original standards they had proposed compositional standards. So something that had a composition of a given amount of heavy metals or whatever was considered hazardous. And while those were in the proposed stage we were asked what the characteristics of our ash were. And then we were turned out of the landfill.[15]

As a result of this reclassification, 3M no longer could dispose of its waste in the Pig's Eye (St. Paul, MN) landfill. In response, 3M wanted to build its own disposal facility but found that it could not because the city of Cottage Grove would not give them the necessary permits.

As a result of these decisions, 3M was temporarily left without a site for disposing of its incinerator ash. In turn, 3M lobbied the legislature to address the hazardous waste problem in the state so that 3M and other Minnesota businesses would be assured of disposal capacity in the future. Business support was instrumental in encouraging the state to address the issue of siting a hazardous waste disposal facility. "The business response back in the early eighties was really a lot of the driving energy behind this siting effort, particularly the major companies like 3M."[16]

Both legislators and members of the Waste Management Board (WMB) were eager to incorporate business interests into the decision-making process. As Lindblom would expect, state officials were concerned about the impact that hazardous waste disposal issues would have on Minnesota's business climate. They were willing to work with business groups to design a strategy that would provide benefits to Minnesota businesses, such as easy and safe disposal of hazardous waste, while attempting to protect Minnesota's environment. This willingness to cooperate with business interests included appointing business representatives to planning and decision-making committees. In addition, the WMB conducted a survey of hazardous waste generators in the state to assess the amount of waste produced and to get recommendations from those generators as to how the state could best serve them.

At the same time, the state worked closely with some important environmental groups, like the Minnesota chapter of the Sierra Club, to develop a plan to resolve Minnesota's hazardous waste problems. At the time of this legislative initiative, the Sierra Club was able to serve as a key representative of environmentalists because it was one of the most politically active environmental groups in the state and the only group with a full-time lobbyist. Through its involvement in the process, the Sierra Club proposed several amendments to the plan developed by the state, and these amendments were incorporated into the final legislation submitted to the legislature for approval.

We have a major interest in seeing that the hazardous waste process that's been established by the legislature is implemented and works. We were deeply involved in the bill; many of the provisions of the bill providing for increased citizen involvement and resource recovery are there because we were representing the environmental interests in the process.[17]

The Sierra Club's strong support for this bill was rooted in their belief that hazardous waste was one of the state's "most pressing environmental problems."[18]

Dee Long, a state representative from Minneapolis and a leader in the passage of the Waste Management Act, summarized the motivation for the legislation by saying:

Back in 1980 the thought was fairly prevalent that there might, in a very short time, not be any facilities available. And therefore, in terms of business development, Minnesota had to come up with some answers. I think that time has proven that is not necessarily the case. But legislators and business interests and environmentalists all thought that it was going to happen. So what came together was an inability to site anything, along with the firm belief that it was absolutely essential to have a disposal facility of some sort in the state. And the pressure created by those two streams, with business and environmental organizations and the legislature working together, led us to pass a bill in a relatively short time period through a number of committees.[19]

Therefore, as those viewing policymaking as dominated by elites would predict, decision-making on hazardous waste issues in Minnesota was made in the context of a policy network in which important interest groups and public officials worked together to design a mutually satisfactory policy. In this case, a small group of legislators with an interest in environmental issues, environmental groups (led most prominently by the Sierra Club), and business interests (led by representatives from 3M) banded together to negotiate a proposal that would be acceptable to all. The cooperation among these elite groups rather than among broad-based and grassroots groups was instrumental in the development of the state's waste management plan.

In 1980 the legislature passed the Waste Management Act. This legislation created the Waste Management Board as the agency responsible for hazardous waste policy in the state. The WMB was charged with conducting a search for the "best" site in the state to locate a hazardous waste landfill. The process was supposed to include widespread public participation, but the final selection of a site was to be based on technical criteria. The state (with the input of citizens) needed to find the safest location for the facility, taking into account soil characteristics, proximity and threat to underground aquifers, and risk to the surrounding population.[20] At the same time, the Waste Management Act authorized the WMB to explore alternatives to traditional landfill disposal. As a way to facilitate public involvement, the WMB conducted public meetings across the state. At these meetings citizens were given an explanation of the geological characteristics of their community and how these would enter into decision-making about a hazardous waste facility. In addition, the overall siting strategy was explained and citizen input was gathered.[21]

As part of the Waste Management Act the legislature established a bipartisan and bicameral oversight committee of hazardous waste policy within the state, called the Legislative Commission on Waste Management (LCWM). This committee was comprised of legislators who were interested in issues of hazardous waste primarily for policy goals.[22] Such committees were typically formed when the legislature faced a problem for which expertise was required and decision-making would be drawn out over a long period of time. Legislators on this committee worked closely with the WMB and developed the skill to outline a viable waste management plan and effectively oversee WMB activities. As a result of the policy orientation of members and the expertise they developed, the LCWM was left alone to decide policy issues with little "interference" from other legislators. As evidence, in the early years of the act, amendments to it were unanimously approved by the legislature upon recommendation by the commission.[23]

The WMB and the LCWM continued to work with organized business and environmental groups as they began the implementation phase of the Waste Management Act. This entailed studying the scope of the hazardous waste problem, determining what type of disposal facility would best serve the state, and finding a site for the disposal facility. As Lowi's assessment of decision-making predicts, the WMB and LCWM were granted considerable leeway in how they addressed the state's problems. They were directed to consider all "feasible and prudent" technologies to reduce the level of waste in the state and to explore different techniques for hazardous waste disposal while looking for a site to locate the new facility.

Businesses supported the strong role that the state elected to play in the siting process through the formation of the Waste Management Board and the use of eminent domain in the final site selection.

> The siting policy should be complete—that is, involve all the necessary public input—but then it should be final so that once they select the site, having gone through all of the public input, then nobody can block the siting by court action, because they have had their input. But then the other thing is then that the state overrule local land-use authority. We wanted that in there.[24]

Businesses like 3M viewed the landfill disposal with a location near the Twin Cities as the best solution. The landfill disposal was also thought to be useful to Minnesota businesses because "with fewer disposal sites available in other states, the cost of hazardous waste disposal for Minnesota firms is becoming increasingly costly—making these firms less competitive."[25] In addition, the Twin Cities location would keep their transportation costs down and provide a relatively cheap and easy way to dispose of their hazardous waste.

Environmental groups continued their endorsement of the Waste Management Act once it was passed by the legislature. The Sierra Club in particular provided strong public backing for the state's siting effort. They recognized that public opposition to the siting effort would arise but felt that it was misguided. In supporting the state's efforts, a representative for the club argued:

> The toughest problem will be to overcome local opposition to the siting of a hazardous waste facility. This is where we [the Sierra Club] can best exert our efforts. If it looks as if all the technological and environmental concerns have been met, we should assist the WMB in overcoming local emotionalism.[26]

In addition, groups like Citizens for a Better Environment and Clean Water Action Coalition were involved in the early stages of the process and generally supported the strategy outlined in the Waste Management Act and implemented by the Waste Management Board.

Despite the general accord among environmental groups, business groups, and state officials over the direction and scope of Minnesota's hazardous waste policy, disagreements among these actors did arise. These differences surfaced in response to the Waste Management Board's *Draft Certificate of Need* report. 3M was emphatic in its belief that a landfill disposal was essential to managing Minnesota's hazardous waste. Discussion of other options, like banning the production of certain wastes or requiring labels telling consumers whether hazardous waste was a by-product of the manufacture of a product, would only antagonize the business community and incite public opposition. In their response to the *Draft Certificate of Need,* 3M argued:

> Rather than present positive approaches to the processing and disposal of hazardous waste, many of the draft report's policies and programs are based on an unnecessarily negative—and in some cases even punitive—attitude. It is difficult to determine how successful this scare tactic approach might be in achieving a significant reduction in the generation of hazardous waste. We have no doubt, however, that it would further discourage new industry from locating in Minnesota, and would be another reason for existing industry to reduce or discontinue operations in Minnesota. Most important, it is at least confusing to the public at the very time success or failure of our Board's mission is at stake. A confused or scared public does little to [e]nsure that success. What's more it is totally unnecessary given current technology and its ability to handle hazardous waste in a safe and sound matter.[27]

Although 3M has a reputation as a leader in environmental protection, in their dealings with Minnesota officials this seemed to lead to a sense that they knew best how to dispose of their waste and an impatience with anything other than landfill disposal. In their view, other options would lead to excessive costs and an unnecessary burden on them.

Likewise, the support of Minnesota's hazardous waste policy by environmental groups was not unequivocal. They expressed some concern that the state was not putting enough pressure on businesses to reduce their hazardous waste output. In hearings regarding the hazardous waste plan devised by the Waste Management Board, Citizens for a Better Environment argued, "Incentives are acceptable when total compliance is not necessary, but regulations are necessary when total compliance is needed—for example, in achieving waste reduction."[28] Another group, Minnesota COACT, objected to the site selection process because the state would use eminent domain to secure a site once an acceptable location was found.[29]

Even though differences arose, the WMB was able to satisfy both business and environmental groups rather than choose among them (as pluralist theory would suggest). Therefore, as Lowi predicts, we cannot necessarily expect interest group mobilization to lead to competition. Instead, interest group mobilization may lead to cooperation and accommodation, as it did in this case. In Minnesota, the state was willing to include language about the importance of waste reduction and reclamation and alternatives to land-fill disposal even though for businesses the need for a landfill disposal was indisputable. At the same time the state negotiated a compromise on public involvement in the process by providing for citizen participation but allowing the final site selection to utilize the state's powers of eminent domain. The use of eminent domain was opposed by some environmental groups, but business leaders were strongly supportive of it.

As specified in the 1980 Waste Management Act, citizens were given an opportunity to evaluate the state's proposals and the potential impact on their community through public hearings. Twenty potential sites were selected across the state, and meetings were held in each of these areas. At these meetings the state's general siting strategy was outlined and citizens were given an opportunity to ask questions and raise concerns. The state viewed this siting strategy as innovative and exhaustive, giving citizens throughout the state information about the siting process and allowing them to respond.

The impact of this public involvement in the direction and strategies that the state was pursuing, however, appears minimal. At the end of public hearings on the draft Hazardous Waste Plan, the Waste Management Board conducted a survey of some of the people in attendance from across the state. Although such a survey cannot be used to reflect public opinion more generally, it does give an overall indication of the responses that the Waste Management Board was receiving from the public on its policy proposals. The survey asked some specific questions regarding the structure of the siting process and the extent to which the state should be involved in and provide financial support for the facility. The results of the policy questions are presented in Table 2.1.

The evidence from this survey highlights important opposition from the public to many of the policies the state was pursuing. The two issues on which citizens expressed a clear opinion were their disapproval of the state's developing its own "integrated" treatment and disposal facility, and their belief that the state should put a higher priority on hazardous waste reduction than on

*Table 2.1* Results from Individual Questionnaires on Policies and Programs

1. Should the state place a higher priority on hazardous waste reduction than on other methods of waste management, such as waste treatment or proper disposal, by concentrating its activities more on encouraging hazardous waste reduction than in developing hazardous waste facilities?
   Yes—85% (231)
   No—9% (23)
   Undecided—6% (18)
2. Should the state develop and operate its own "integrated" hazardous waste facility, including disposal, treatment, and temporary waste storage?
   Yes—22% (59)
   No—67% (183)
   Undecided—11% (29)

*Number of respondents in parentheses.
Source: Kevin Johnson, Assistant Information Officer, Waste Management Board, Memorandum to Board Members and Staff Regarding the Waste Management Board's Citizen Questionnaire, 6 December, 1983, Waste Management Board Records, State Historical Archives, Minnesota State Historical Society.

disposal and treatment. Despite the preferences of citizens given at the hearings and reiterated in the survey, the state continued to pursue policies that citizens opposed. For example, citizens clearly preferred that the state make waste reduction a higher priority than waste disposal, but the WMB spent far more of its resources on disposal than on waste reduction. In addition, notwithstanding public opposition to the state's developing its own treatment and disposal facility, this is exactly what the state proposed in its 1986 amendments to the Waste Management Act. The results of this survey suggest that the public had little impact on the structure of the state's policy.

Indeed, the Waste Management Board made it clear that it did not want to appear too beholden to public pressures and easily swayed by public opinion. For example, the WMB examined crystalline bedrock disposal in some of the granite formations in northern Minnesota as an alternative to traditional landfill disposal. This technique involved drilling into granite cavities so that hazardous waste could be pumped in and stored until a permanent disposal process was developed. Public opposition to this proposal was very strong, particularly in the Ash Lake area of St. Louis County. Eventually the WMB abandoned this siting strategy but wanted to make it clear that public opposition had little or nothing to do with their decision. One of the board members, Keith Kuitters, told reporters "that he abstained [in the voting to abandon this strategy] because he feared that voting to drop the four bedrock sites might be interpreted by the public as bowing to political pressures."[30] Other board members argued that the crystalline bedrock disposal process was too costly to be justified at that time.

Other state officials also displayed some skepticism that citizen involvement was essential to the process. When the state was examining crystalline bedrock disposal, one state official responded to charges that the Waste Management Board was making biased assessments and performing a "less than competent job" by saying:

> The Waste Management Act envisioned that citizens should assist in making these tough decisions. The real unanswered question is whether or not participants from the site areas can look beyond their parochial viewpoints and consider what is best for the entire state. Can they participate from a constructive viewpoint rather than being totally negative and obstructionist? Can they objectively listen, learn, and reason with their counterparts who are all working on this problem together? It would be unfortunate if we as participants decide to solidify the "we" and "they" or an "us against them" mentality and waste most of our effort trying to confuse and derail each other. . . . *If we cannot work together, future opportunities for citizens to make decisions in controversial issues may not be available.* What we need are facts, regardless of whether they support or do not support the use of crystalline bedrock for hazardous waste disposal. (emphasis added)[31]

Implicit in this threat that citizens must cooperate is the notion that participation is a privilege that can be taken away. In addition, this statement reveals that state officials saw the hazardous waste issue as a technical one that could be decided according to the facts rather than as a political choice about whether the facility was necessary and who should bear any risk associated with it.[32]

## The Rise of Citizen Opposition

By 1984 the WMB narrowed the number of sites to four communities. As site selection became more concrete, opposition within the selected communities became quite intense. In Carver County, near the Twin Cities, a group called Minnesota People Opposed to Wasting Earth's Resources (MN-Power) formed to try to stop the state from testing sites in the county as a candidate for the hazardous waste facility. They fought the state in the courts, trying to keep state officials off private land to impede the testing process. Their opposition to the siting effort centered around the state's ability to exercise its power of eminent domain in selecting a site. They were particularly troubled by the thought of the state "taking" farmland from productive farmers. In addition, they believed that recycling the wastes produced in the state would sufficiently reduce the waste stream so that hazardous waste disposal within Minnesota's borders would not be necessary.

Similar grassroots opposition groups formed, like Minnesota Future Agricultural Interests Recognized (MN-Fair) and Minnesota North (an organization of residents from the northern part of the state), and worked to oppose the siting of a hazardous waste facility in the counties outside of the metro area.[33] By staging protests and taking the state to court, grassroots interest groups like MN-Power were able to draw into question the need for the facility in the minds of some legislators. Eventually Senator Ronald Dicklich of Hibbing, Minnesota, conceded, "We spent millions and millions on this siting process without really knowing what we need."[34]

As a result of these protests by constituents in the districts under consideration, their elected representatives were alerted to problems with the decision-making process and undertook steps to correct them. Initially there were moves within the legislature to try to dismantle the Waste Management Board and end the siting effort altogether. However, supporters of the process tried to push through amendments to the Waste Management Act that preserved the Waste Management Board but asked for a moratorium on siting to reevaluate the need for the facility. The amendments were proposed by Dee Long, one of the strong supporters of siting a hazardous waste facility, who argued that the original bill "tends to treat Minnesota as an island. (The Amendments) would allow us to look at available facilities out of the state."[35] Therefore, once opposition mounted, even strong supporters of a new facility in the state were willing to consider the possibility that Minnesota could continue to use out-of-state landfills and not site the facility.

However, for most within the policy network—members of the Legislative Commission on Waste Management, staff members of the Waste Management Board, and the influential business and environmental groups—reconsideration of the issues was merely evidence that the legislature had lost its resolve. Likewise, consideration of a moratorium on the siting process was opposed by businesses. Kenneth Ford of Honeywell wrote to encourage the WMB and the LCWM to find a state site for hazardous waste disposal and to voice his concerns about Minnesota businesses continuing to rely on out-of-state facilities.

> Exercising this option [relying on out-of-state facilities], we believe, would be a dangerous course and would only exacerbate the already poor competitive posture Minnesota businesses have with other states that are meeting this need. Additionally, we believe this option might encourage retaliatory actions by other states as well as create a greater potential for improper treatment and disposal of hazardous waste generated in our borders.[36]

Businesses remained firmly committed to landfill disposal as the solution to Minnesota's hazardous waste problem.

Yet, despite the protests of those who had worked to design the state's hazardous waste policy, in 1984 the Minnesota legislature approved a bill calling for a moratorium on the current siting process. The bill required the Waste Management Board to reassess the need for this facility by conducting a statewide assessment of the amount and types of waste. In addition, WMB personnel were authorized to explore alternative technologies to landfill disposal. Once these tasks were completed, the WMB would recommend whether a facility could be built to handle the state's waste while operating at a price that was economically competitive with existing disposal alternatives.

The approval of the moratorium by state legislators at the behest of their constituents demonstrates that citizens can in fact influence decision-making on public policies, even in the context of elite policy networks. The plan negotiated among environmental groups, business groups, and state officials, and eventually approved by the state legislature, fell victim to citizen opposition. Citizens were able to draw their legislators' attention to the hazardous waste issues and the action taken by the WMB in its siting efforts. Although this "fire-alarm" strategy of legislative oversight does provide some modicum of political control over the process, it is limited to curbing the *capacity* of state officials and their interest group allies to pursue the policies which they had negotiated. It does not ensure citizen involvement in the formative stages of the process and allow them to help direct the course the state will take.

## A New Direction—Stabilization and Containment

The moratorium had important implications for the structure of future decision-making on hazardous waste policy. Despite their obvious dissatisfaction with the first siting attempt, the legislature as a whole sent the issue back to the "experts" on the WMB and the LCWM for reconsideration. The failure of the first siting effort led to a breakdown of the consensus that had been worked out among business groups, environmental groups, and state officials. The new policymaking context, in fact, put greater reliance on the state's problem-solving resources as a way to resolve the political problems encountered in the previous siting effort. As this section will show, the breakdown of the policy network through mobilized citizen opposition had the unexpected consequence of enhancing the autonomy of the WMB, as state officials worked to devise a solution that they believed would best serve the interests of business, environmental, and citizen groups.

The pursuit of a voluntary process and the stabilization and containment facility can be seen as examples of policy innovation and entrepreneurship (see Berry and Berry 1990; Gray 1973; Walker 1969; Schneider et al. 1995; Mintrom 1997). Waste management officials looked around in other states and eventually in Canada for a model of successful siting. Given the inability of states to site disposal facilities, it is not surprising that they looked to the successful siting of a stabilization and containment facility in Swan Hills, Alberta. Minnesota state officials examined this case thoroughly and incorporated the lessons from Swan Hills into their recommendations to the state legislature about how to proceed.

In 1986 the WMB came back to the legislature with its Estimate of Need report. In summarizing the results from the report, Ken Stabler—one of its authors—argued:

> You may not need it tomorrow, you may not need it five years from now, but given the timeframe necessary to site and build a facility, you couldn't wait until you really needed it. . . . We weren't in a crisis, but the long-term planning required that there needed to be a facility.[37]

In the report, the WMB argued that Minnesota industry produced significant amounts of inorganic wastes. The inorganic wastes were comprised primarily of heavy metals, most of which were the by-product of chrome-plating processes and the ash from 3M's waste incineration plant in Cottage

Grove. The WMB proposed a hazardous waste stabilization and containment facility as a means to cope with Minnesota's inorganic hazardous waste. The stabilization and containment facility would provide an alternative to traditional landfill disposal. The process involved mixing the waste with concrete and forming hazardous waste capsules which could be entombed in a containment facility. The containment facility would be built above the soil level so that the facility could be monitored and corrective action taken if leaks were detected. The WMB believed that the 15,000 tons of inorganic waste produced annually in the state justified the construction of this hazardous waste facility and that the $20 million facility could be built and operated at a price that would make it competitive with the alternatives available to Minnesota businesses.[38]

In its 1986 report, the Waste Management Board also recommended that the state abandon the four sites remaining from the first phase of the siting process, and outlined a voluntary siting process. The WMB sought and won legislative approval of this change in the siting process in the 1986 legislative session. Under the voluntary process any county in the state could volunteer as a candidate for the hazardous waste facility if a majority of county board members approved and agreed to send a statement of interest to the WMB. In exchange for volunteering, counties would receive $4,000 per month. The money was allocated to help counties finance their own evaluation of the facility for their community. (However, the money was placed in the general revenue fund for the county, and counties were not required to use the money for evaluative purposes.) The WMB strongly believed that such an approach would minimize public opposition and ultimately secure a site for the state.

According to the amendments to the Waste Management Act, each interested county first had to establish a Citizen's Advisory Committee made up of citizens from the county. This committee had to study the issue and recommend to the county board whether the facility and compensation package would be economically beneficial and socially desirable for the county. If the advisory committee recommended that the county proceed, a final site within the county would be selected by the WMB and a technical evaluation would be undertaken to ensure that the facility could be safely built and operated. Finally, the counties would negotiate a contract with the WMB, subject to funding authorization by the legislature. The terms of the contract were not specified in the 1986 legislation. Therefore the WMB and the counties proceeded under the assumption that many forms of compensation were available, including a residential tax credit for county residents, a business tax credit for county businesses, and capital and technical assistance for a new county solid waste landfill.[39]

With the passage of this new legislation, much of the support for the facility within the legislature eroded. Although members of the LCWM voted to move forward with the voluntary process, it was not enthusiastically endorsed. State Representative Dee Long, a member of the LCWM, claimed, "Oh no, the voluntary process, I never thought it was a good idea. Why not try it if you think it is a good idea? I never assumed that would work. But if people [the WMB] thought that it would, let them try."[40] Likewise, Senator Gene Merriam, the author of the Waste Management Act, was doubtful that the voluntary process would succeed. "I had been and remain skeptical that it will ever work but said that it might be worth the effort."[41]

This weak endorsement of the voluntary process left the WMB with little legislative oversight and considerable latitude in decision-making. The new policy proposal broke down the close relationship between the WMB and the LCWM. The ability of the WMB to pursue its siting plan with the halfhearted support of the legislature underscores the resiliency and independence of administrative power.

Despite the reluctance on the part of legislators to stand firmly behind this siting effort, the WMB remained committed to the voluntary process and to the stabilization and containment facility. According to them, this facility would provide better protection for Minnesota's environment, since the hazardous waste would be treated and stabilized prior to disposal. This would reduce the chances of contaminating the ground around the site as well as underground aquifers near the site. The WMB also believed that it was anticipating stricter disposal guidelines that would be promulgated in the future. Despite these benefits, the WMB conceded that with the amount of waste produced in the state, the facility was only marginally economically viable[42] (but important to the environment). The facility would lose money the first few years, until the lack of alternative disposal options increased the price and made stabilization and containment competitive with landfill disposal.[43]

According to state theorists, when state officials are operating with a certain amount of autonomy, they will be motivated both by eagerness to bring their expertise to bear on policy issues and by pressures they receive from those above them in the administrative structure (Skocpol 1985; Nordlinger 1981). In this case, the Minnesota Waste Management Board was receptive to the construction of a facility in the state because of its subordinate role to the EPA on hazardous waste matters. With the passage of the 1980 Comprehensive Environmental Response, Compensation and Liability Act (CERCLA), states were required to develop a Capacity Assurance Plan which would ensure that the state could manage the hazardous waste produced within its borders for the next twenty years. Once completed, the plans were sent to the Environmental Protection Agency for review and approval.[44] Although there was some uncertainty about what the EPA's sanctions would be if a state did not establish an adequate plan, decision-makers in Minnesota, as in most other states, were concerned that the EPA might carry through on its threat to withdraw Superfund money from those states that failed to meet the planning requirements.[45] Jack Ditmore of Minnesota's Environmental Quality Board wrote, "Assurance of capacity will soon be required for states to continue to obtain federal funds to clean up Superfund sites."[46]

Although under pressure to comply with the EPA's mandate to develop a Capacity Assurance Plan, states were granted latitude in how they would best meet these requirements. The EPA (and state officials around the country) was concerned about the future availability of disposal facilities and hoped that some states would pursue siting a hazardous waste facility as a means of managing their hazardous waste into the future. However, Minnesota officials recognized that "a state can assure adequate capacity by showing that its waste can be managed either within the state or under a cooperative agreement with other states."[47] Therefore siting a facility was not required for developing a Capacity Assurance Plan.

Although they clearly recognized that siting a facility was not required of them, state officials believed that going through the siting process would help them develop a Capacity Assurance Plan and that their plan might be more favorably viewed by the EPA if they tried to site a facility. Neil Miller, Public Affairs Officer of the WMB, reported:

For example, continuing the siting program here, it [pressure from the federal government] created a much stronger incentive to continue our siting program here, just so that we could meet those capacity assurance requirements. It became another reason to move forward with this. That way we could work with other states and say, "We've got this [program] that we are working on." And that can count toward our Capacity Assurance Plan.[48]

In fact, in the Capacity Assurance Plan that the state submitted in October 1989, the state listed its attempts to site a hazardous waste facility as part of its efforts to manage the state's waste over the next twenty years.[49]

In addition, as part of its Capacity Assurance Plan, Minnesota hoped to negotiate agreements with other states as a strategy for developing an integrated waste management plan. The facility could be used in waste exchange programs with other states.

> Minnesota could agree to accept limited quantities of waste from cooperating states for stabilization and containment in return for assurance that Minnesota waste generators will have access to other types of waste management facilities in cooperating states.[50]

It was therefore important for the state to get the host county to allow out-of-state waste to be accepted by the facility.[51]

Finally, federal regulations on the proper disposal of hazardous waste had some bearing on Minnesota's decision-making since state officials believed that federal regulations might impose stricter guidelines in the future. They feared that those stricter guidelines would result in the closing of existing disposal facilities and might leave Minnesota waste generators without safe disposal options.

> Considering the difficulty of siting new facilities of any type, disposal capacity cannot be taken for granted, and new EPA requirements to upgrade facilities will likely increase tipping fees significantly and perhaps cause some existing facilities to close.[52]

At the same time, state officials were confident that new federal regulations would require disposal techniques other than landfill disposal. This was a justification, in their minds, for proceeding with the stabilization and containment facility rather than landfill disposal. They tried to persuade the business community that they were anticipating future regulations, and with a stabilization and containment facility in place, the state would be in a good position to manage waste in the future.

State theorists and students of bureaucracy argue that in addition to the pressures state actors receive from their superiors, the prevailing ideology of these state officials and the institutional norms and goals they develop will orient them to particular types of solutions (Krasner 1978; Heclo 1974). In studying hazardous waste policy in Minnesota, therefore, we would expect the prevailing worldview and the goals of WMB personnel to help explain policymaking in the context of administrative autonomy.

The perception among state officials was that this facility was essential to protecting Minnesota's environment in the long run. Neil Miller, Public Affairs Officer of the Waste Management Board, argued, "We've always seen our role as to make sure that the environment benefits, that this becomes part of an integrated system in Minnesota—waste reduction and recycling."[53] Likewise, Terri Port, Director of Facility Development, argued that

> the long-term benefits that could be provided to industry and all state residents may easily outweigh what appear to be large short-term costs. I would prefer to pay now, because to pay later assumes that you can fix any damage that you might do through improper management of hazardous waste. I would prefer to pay up front for what looks like a gold-plated hazardous waste management facility. Then I would have a very, very small chance of having problems in the future.[54]

Coupled with this sense of responsibility, state officials saw themselves to some extent as guardians of Minnesota's future as well as its tradition of progressive policymaking. Siting this facility would help the state become a national leader in hazardous waste disposal. "The successful development and operation of a stabilization and containment facility could set an important precedent for future siting efforts in regard to both environmental protection and social acceptability."[55] Joseph Pavelich, Chair of the Waste Management Board, echoed these sentiments:

> The purpose behind building this plant is to safely treat hazardous industrial waste generated by Minnesota companies instead of sending it to other states for disposal in landfills. Because of the high standards that Minnesota has set for this facility, it will be more protective of the environment than any existing or planned waste treatment facility anywhere.[56]

This forward-looking tradition served as an important justification for the stabilization and containment facility despite little support from key environmental and business groups.

Environmental damage has occurred in the past at waste management facilities because industry and government have merely responded to existing problems instead of anticipating them. . . . By combining the practical, hands-on knowledge of these companies with the insights of state experts working in the public interest, the design, construction and operation of this facility will be proactive instead of reactive.[57]

In addition, state officials perceived themselves as having an obligation to properly dispose of Minnesota's hazardous waste. Neil Miller of the Waste Management Board noted:

I've noticed in my time that there is almost a moral dimension to this. We've sometimes found ourselves making the argument that we [Minnesotans] are making these inorganic residual wastes and taking them to other states. But we should be taking care of that ourselves. We should be responsible for our own waste.[58]

Based on archival research and interviews, it appears that state officials developed a complex ideology in which they saw themselves as having a responsibility to protect Minnesota's environment, preserve Minnesota's tradition of progressive policymaking, and ensure a healthy future for subsequent generations of Minnesotans. These commitments were interwoven with their goal to ensure that hazardous waste policy would not jeopardize the state's business climate. Their pursuit of these goals led them to consider the construction of a stabilization and containment facility despite little obvious support from societal groups.

Business interests balked at this new strategy of using a voluntary process to site a stabilization and containment facility. 3M in particular believed that the WMB was going too far in trying to assuage public fears. They wanted a facility that would be below ground level, as in landfill disposal, not above-ground storage, as proposed in the stabilization and containment facility. "Our position, 3M and industry generally, was initially in opposition to this, because there are reasons that you would want to put it below-ground. You have better stability as far as support of the material."[59]

In addition, 3M believed that the state "overreacted" in pursuing the stabilization and containment facility. They thought the WMB was being unnecessarily cautious in using disposal techniques that far surpassed the level of safety required by federal law. These new methods would increase the price of disposal for Minnesota's facility so that it would not be competitive with currently available options like landfill disposal. For 3M, one of the largest potential users of this facility, the projected costs were three and a half times as much as with their current landfill disposal vendors.[60]

> The agency [the WMB], their argument is that the requirement for stabilization is something that is coming, that it is something that will be required elsewhere. And that may be true. But still I have difficulty going to my management and saying, "Okay, you guys are spending a million dollars a year for ash disposal, and I want you to start using the Minnesota facility and that's going to cost you three and half million." They say, "Why should we do that?" And I say, "Because you are Minnesota industry and you should support this." Baloney, that doesn't fly.[61]

3M also expressed opposition to the voluntary process. Their resistance stemmed from their desire to have the facility located in the metropolitan area so that transportation costs would be minimized. The voluntary process would make it unlikely that a metro site would be developed because the amount of money available for economic development was insufficient to induce the most populated and prosperous counties in the state to volunteer. From the perspective of 3M, this created two problems. First, having a rural site would provide little reduction in transportation costs since 3M could ship its waste to Illinois for about the same price that they could send it to a site in rural Minnesota. "Red Lake [one of the volunteer counties] suffers from the problem that, from our perspective, it is almost as far away from Minneapolis-St. Paul as Chicago is. From that standpoint, you really have no advantage."[62] In addition, they recognized that a rural site would be unpopular because it would put the facility into direct conflict with agricultural land use. The same geological conditions, like a deep clay base under the top soil, make for both good farmland and a good hazardous waste site.[63]

Other business voiced opposition to a stabilization and containment facility because it would put the state in direct competition with some existing private recycling and reclamation businesses. Metro Recovery Systems (MRS), a metal reprocessing business in Roseville, Minnesota (a suburb of the Twin Cities), argued that part of the state's new facility would compete with its own treatment of industrial hazardous waste. Both facilities would recover metal from hazardous waste generated in processes like metal plating. In a letter to state Senator Robert Lessard, Dan Shuster, President of Metropolitan Recovery Corporation, wrote:

> Given the questionable economics of the proposed state owned facility, and the assumption that MRS would be one of the two primary customers of the facility, it behooves the legislature to find out what we think. Our facility has the potential to handle all of the materials that need stabilization in Minnesota and we are on record as opposing the development of a containment facility that has precipitation and stabilization processing tagged on to make the deal more attractive to out-of-state developers. Such an operation is capacity-redundant with our operation and puts the state in direct competition with existing private enterprise.[64]

MRS was concerned that the state would subsidize its treatment fees to make its facility run near capacity, thus undercutting MRS's business.[65]

At the same time that Minnesota businesses became disenchanted with the siting process, the support of environmental groups waned. Whereas businesses sensed that the reformulation of the siting strategy was not to their benefit, environmental groups feared that businesses might get too good a deal through state subsidies for waste disposal. Environmental groups like the Clean Water Action Committee and Preserve Our Land were concerned that 3M could negotiate favorable terms for using the facility since roughly 30 percent of the inorganic hazardous waste in the state was the ash from 3M's Chemolite waste incineration facility.[66] The state needed businesses like 3M to use the facility if it was going to be economically viable.[67]

Environmental groups were also concerned that by building the facility the WMB would face disincentives to push for additional waste reduction in Minnesota. These groups believed that the state needed 15,000 tons of waste a year to make the facility economically viable, and if it reduced the waste stream significantly through waste reduction programs, the facility would operate at a loss. Alternatively, Minnesota could import waste to make up the difference in tonnage. However, both of these scenarios were a concern to environmental groups because neither importing waste nor promoting stabilization and containment would help reduce Minnesota's waste stream and they might in fact increase the amount of waste disposed of in the state.

Throughout this phase of the policy process the state consistently defended its advocacy of the stabilization and containment facility, in part by claiming it was best for Minnesota in the long run. Neil Miller of the Waste Management Board argued, "[T]his facility would have so many features—safety features, environmental protection features—as part of it and would be very attractive to industry in Minnesota because of liability questions."[68]

The state insisted that the facility would reduce the liability costs of Minnesota business in the long run because it would be designed so safely. The state believed that in the future the EPA would impose stricter regulations on the disposal of hazardous waste and because the stabilization and containment facility would meet future regulatory requirements, Minnesota business would be protected from regulatory innovations. Since this facility was less likely to have problems than a landfill, it would also reduce the likelihood that Minnesota businesses would be involved in litigation to pay for environmental damages. Therefore, in the minds of public officials, the additional safety of this facility justified the higher costs.

As testimony to the state's commitment to this facility and its interest in making it economically viable, in 1988 the legislature, at the request of the WMB, approved a bill that would provide public ownership of the facility but it would be run by a private waste management company. Part of the rationale for public ownership was to alleviate citizens' concerns that market incentives would lead a firm to cut corners on safety in pursuit of profits.[69] In addition, the state argued that the facility was not economically viable, given the price of alternative disposal strategies, but by subsidizing the facility in the short term and waiting until disposal capacity became scarce, it could make a profit over the lifetime of the facility.[70] Also, because the state was involved in the issue it could purchase additional insurance for the facility to pay claims in the event of an accident. (The developer was required to have an insurance policy that would provide a minimum of $40 million of protection.) This would allow the state to have some role in liability, and that would benefit business in the long run. As owner, the state could help businesses that used the facility avoid being left in a situation in which one or two big producers ended up being the "deep pockets." With joint and several liability, large corporations who have the ability to pay for all of the damages become likely targets for litigation in the event of environmental degradation from a facility.

The political, economic, and environmental factors that led state officials to view the hazardous waste facility as essential to Minnesota's hazardous waste policy coincided with a somewhat suspicious view of the role that citizens should play in the process. Although decision-making did include the public at various points in the process, citizens who opposed the facility were generally seen as misinformed and in need of education on the issue. For example, when two counties withdrew as candidates for the facility, Joseph Pavelich, Chair of the Waste Management Board, argued that such action

> illustrates the need for an increased level of public understanding about the issues. We are increasing our public education efforts to overcome some misconceptions about the facility, but for many people it's still very easy to say "not in my backyard," instead of learning about the issues and working with us toward a solution.[71]

Likewise, Neil Miller of the WMB contended that citizens generally have a "visceral" response to hazardous waste projects and need to be better informed about the issue. The implication is that if the "facts" are presented to the citizens in the county, they will think like the state officials and recognize the need for and safety of the facility.

Despite the resolve on the part of the WMB to pursue the stabilization and containment facility even in the face of substantial opposition, and the willingness on the part of the legislature to let them continue, the WMB had limited coercive capacity to achieve its objectives. Though it had gained a good deal of autonomy on hazardous waste decision-making, the WMB had only limited means by which it could pursue these goals. For example, it was important for the state to get 3M to commit to the facility since it was a major waste producer in the state and its waste was factored into the economic viability of the facility. However, 3M had the upper hand in negotiations with the state on hazardous waste issues because it had operations in many states across the country and therefore could bargain effectively with many states, not just Minnesota.

If the state had sited the facility, it would have had to induce the support of businesses since it could not mandate their disposal in the Minnesota facility. Because the state had a pressing need for 3M to use the facility, environmental groups were concerned that 3M would have the upper hand in negotiations with the state once the facility was built. 3M refused to commit to the facility prior to its being completed and the final tipping fees being determined. Environmental groups were concerned that either the state would need to import waste from other states to make the stabilization and containment facility economically viable or the state would strike a deal with 3M to get them to use the facility. The environmental groups feared that the state would discount its price to 3M to get its waste and/or would work out an arrangement with 3M to shield it from some or all of its liability.[72]

At the same time, the state's reliance on the voluntary process rather than eminent domain meant that it must also induce cooperation from citizens. Under the voluntary process counties could negotiate contracts with the state to arrive at a level of compensation which would satisfy both parties. However, under this siting strategy the state could not mandate that a county accept the facility; it had to gain their cooperation through the promise of money and other forms of compensation. Counties could withdraw from the siting process simply by a majority vote of the county commissioners.

Thus, despite the latitude that the WMB enjoyed in designing and pursuing its vision of Minnesota's hazardous waste policy, its ability to effectively implement its plan was constrained. Only through the use of monetary inducements could it gain the cooperation of both waste generators who would be using the facility and citizens from the community in which the facility would be sited. In this case, a high degree of state autonomy coincided with relatively weak coercive capacity. The state was left with weak capacity because legislators were reluctant to grant the use of the state's powers of eminent domain a second time and risk further outrage from their constituents.

## Conclusion

What emerges from this analysis has important implications for our understanding of the Nimby syndrome. The first and perhaps most interesting finding from this analysis is the way in which the Nimby syndrome itself entered into the debate. It is generally seen as an analytic tool to describe the opposition of citizens, but as this case shows, it can also be used as a means to discredit opposition. When citizens began to oppose the state's siting effort, WMB officials claimed that their opposition was overly emotional and efforts were made to correct what they saw as misperceptions and naïveté on the part of citizens.

Citizens' role in Minnesota's hazardous waste policymaking can best be described as decentralized and reactive. Early in the process elite policy networks developed among business groups, environmental groups, and state officials. These actors were instrumental in setting priorities and designing solutions to Minnesota's hazardous waste problems. The state was willing to bargain and negotiate with these elite interest groups to accommodate their preferences and at the same time ignore some of the citizens' concerns about disposal and state involvement in siting. However, the important influence of these policy elites in the beginning stages was eventually negated through the rise of citizen opposition in candidate communities and citizens' appeals to their legislators to reconsider the siting effort as mandated in the original Waste Management Act. As a result of citizen mobilization, the plans that resulted from elite policy negotiations were rejected and some measure of political control of the process was sustained. Yet, because they were not part of the early negotiations, citizens were left with this obstructionist role.

This history of Minnesota's policymaking also reveals the complex ways in which state officials can control policy. Initially, they did not meet the technocratic ideal in which state officials make and implement policy isolated from external political pressures. They knew that they needed the support of influential businesses and environmental groups to site the landfill. Surprisingly, citizens' ability to disrupt the policy network enhanced state autonomy over decision-making rather than eroding it. After the initial siting effort was suspended, legislators turned to the experts within the Waste Management Board to devise a solution which would best meet Minnesota's environmental and business interests and have some hope of overcoming citizen opposition. Therefore, under conditions of political stalemate and a history of failed policy implementation, state autonomy can be enhanced as elected officials turn to policy experts to resolve political conflict.

In gaining this autonomy, policymaking by state officials became more influenced by internal pressures and norms than by the external demands of elite interest groups. This autonomy arose, however, without the coercive capacity that is often attributed to the modern state. In relying on the voluntary process to site the stabilization and containment facility, the Waste Management Board was left without the powers of eminent domain that were included in the initial siting attempt. Successful siting was dependent on the WMB's using its powers of inducement and persuasion to gain citizen cooperation in the siting process. Counties that volunteered would be offered compensation in exchange for accepting the site, and the WMB would use its technical expertise to convince citizens of the importance and safety of this facility. Therefore even though the state lacked coercive capacity to force citizens to cooperate, it maintained important technical and financial resources to induce their cooperation. State officials could use these resources in an effort to gain the consent of citizens for its policy preferences. The development of the state's noncoercive capacity and its implications for hazardous waste siting and our understanding of the Nimby syndrome are developed further in the next chapter.

## Notes

1. Although definitions of democracy and democratic institutions are always partial and contestable, in this research project I am particularly interested in the extent to which citizens can exercise self-governance in policymaking, either indirectly through their representatives or directly through participation in policy decisions.

2. Theda Skocpol, "Bringing the State Back In: Strategies of Analysis in Current Research," in *Bringing the State Back In,* eds. Peter Evans, Dietrich Reuschemeyer, and Theda Skocpol (New York: Cambridge University Press, 1985), 3–43; Stephen Krasner, *Defending the National Interest: Raw Material Investments and US Foreign Policy* (Princeton: Princeton University Press, 1978). The term "policy network" is taken from Hugh Heclo, *Modern Social Politics in Britain and Sweden* (New Haven: Yale University Press, 1974).

3. Matthew D. McCubbins and Thomas Schwartz, "Congressional Oversight Overlooked: Police Patrol and Fire Alarms," *American Journal of Political Science* 28 (February 1984): 165–179.

4. Influential groups are not likely to need legislators' help in gaining access to administrative decisions, but weaker, grassroots groups and citizens will need to appeal to their representatives to have input in policymaking.

5. These studies contend that there is a "stimulus-response" model in which legislators' preferences (the stimulus) are translated into bureaucratic action (the response). As this analysis will show, a simple model of stimulus-response does not fully account for the discretion and latitude that bureaucrats have in their relationship with legislators.

6. Skocpol, "Bringing the State Back In," and Theda Skocpol and Kenneth Finegold, "State Capacity and Economic Intervention in the Early New Deal," *Political Science Quarterly* 97 (May 1982) : 255–277.

7. Krasner, *Defending the National Interest.*

8. United States Environmental Protection Agency, 1979, *Siting of Hazardous Waste Management Facilities and Public Opposition: Final Report,* report prepared by Centaur Associates, Inc., 191.

9. Ibid.

10. Ibid., 193.

11. Ibid., 191.

12. 3M is the second largest publicly held company in Minnesota, based on a measure of revenues, and the third largest in terms of number of employees. Honeywell, which also played an important role in the early discussions about waste management, is the fourth largest publicly held company based on a measure of revenues and in terms of number of employees (Corporate Report 1991).

13. Senator Gene Merriam, Minnesota State Senate, interview with author, St. Paul, Minnesota, 16 July 1990.

14. Ibid.; Representative Dee Long, Minnesota State Representative, interview with author, St. Paul, Minnesota, 7 July 1990.

15. Russ Susag, Environmental Officer 3M Corporation, interview with author, St. Paul, Minnesota, 30 June 1990.

16. Neil Miller, Public Affairs Officer, Minnesota Waste Management Board, interview with author, St. Paul, Minnesota, 29 April 1990.

At the time the Waste Management Act was under consideration, 3M took a more active role in lobbying for this legislation than other business interests.

At a time when virtually every other industry looked to keeping a public distance on any hazardous waste issues, 3M was an up front and strong advocate of necessary legislative activity that would lead to this state facing up to its hazardous waste responsibilities. As part of this effort 3M supported the Minnesota Waste Management Act and worked actively for its passage by the state legislature in 1980. (*Draft Certificate of Need* 1984)

17. Chuck Dayton, Sierra Club Lobbyist, interview in the *Sierra North Star,* June 1980, 3.

18. Ibid.

19. Representative Dee Long, Minnesota State Representative, interview with author, St. Paul, Minnesota, 7 July 1990.

20. Waste Management Act, 1980, (MN 155A.193).

21. Minnesota Waste Management Board, 1981, *Charting a Course: Public Participation in the Siting of Hazardous Waste Facilities,* Crystal, Minnesota.

22. Senator Gene Merriam, Minnesota State Senator, interview with author, St. Paul, Minnesota, 16 July 1990; Representative Dee Long, Minnesota State Representative, interview with author, St. Paul, Minnesota, 7 July 1990.

That policy goals motivated these legislators to address hazardous waste policy is consistent with Fenno's findings about legislators at the national level (Fenno 1973). This case shows, however, that policy-oriented legislators can work with other state actors to form policy networks (Heclo 1974). These networks function to serve the policy interests of legislators and state actors rather than the more immediate goals of constituents. Therefore legislators are sometimes part of democratic political control but sometimes part of the state's administrative apparatus.

23. Sue Robertson, Legislative Assistant to the Legislative Commission on Waste Management, interview with author, St. Paul, Minnesota, 7 July 1990.

24. Russ Susag, Environmental Officer 3M Corporation, interview with author, St. Paul, Minnesota, 30 June 1990.

25. Minnesota Waste Management Board, 1984, *Draft Certificate of Need,* St. Paul, Minnesota.

26. Dennis Lindeke, "The Hazardous Waste Problem in Minnesota," *Sierra North Star,* February 1981, 7.

It is interesting (and surprising) that the Sierra Club adopted this skeptical attitude toward citizen participation, since they had in fact argued for including it in the Waste Management Act. This apparent reversal in attitude is partly explained by the fact that urban environmentalists worked with the WMB to develop the siting plan, and rural groups mobilized opposition.

27. Minnesota Waste Management Board, 1984, *Draft Certificate of Need,* St. Paul, Minnesota, IX-H6.

28. Report on the 16 January 1984 Public Hearing on the Waste Management Board's *Draft Hazardous Waste Management Plan and Certificate of Need,* Waste Management Board Records, State Archives, Minnesota Historical Society, 16.

29. Ibid., 31.

30. Dean Rebuffoni, "State Ends Search for Below-Ground Waste Storage Site," *Minneapolis Star and Tribune,* 24 February 1984, 4B.

31. Letter from Tom Johnson to John Essame, 12 December 1983, Waste Management Board Records, State Archives, Minnesota Historical Society, 31.

32. Matheny and Williams (1988) and Rosenbaum (1983) argue that there is a perception among state administrators that citizens are only to be informed about the issue, not that they have substantive information to contribute. In addition, in a survey of state administrators and chemical officials, Davis (1984–1985) found that respondents showed little interest in citizen participation.

33. Dan Oberdorfer, "Group Fighting to Keep Waste Site out of Carver County," *Minneapolis Star and Tribune,* 27 March 1983, B3.

34. Bill Salisbury and Allen Short, "Moratorium Set on Hazardous Waste Site Search," *St. Paul Pioneer,* 25 April 1984, 10A.

35. Dean Rebuffoni and Jim Dawson, "Proposals May End Search for Waste Dump in State," *Minneapolis Star and Tribune,* 16 March 1984, 3B.

36. Letter from Kenneth G. Ford, Corporate Manager, Environmental Affairs, Honeywell Corporation, to Richard Dunn, Chair of the Waste Management Board, 17 January 1984, Waste Management Board Records, State Historical Archives, Minnesota Historical Society.

37. Ken Stabler, Acting Director of Facility Development, Waste Management Board, interview with author, Minneapolis, Minnesota, 20 June 1990.

38. Minnesota Waste Management Board, 1988, *Stabilization and Containment: Report on Facility Development,* St. Paul, Minnesota.

39. For details, see "Koochiching County Contract," Koochiching County, Minnesota, 1989.

40. Representative Dee Long, Minnesota State Representative, interview with author, St. Paul, Minnesota, 7 July 1990.

41. Senator Gene Merriam, Minnesota State Senator, interview with author, St. Paul, Minnesota, 16 July 1990.

42. Minnesota Waste Management Board, 1988, *Stabilization and Containment: Report on Facility Development,* St. Paul, Minnesota, 140.

43. Memorandum, Terri Ann Port to Hazardous Waste Planning Council, "Summary of Issues Regarding Facility Development Program," 3 March 1989, 2.

44. Minnesota Waste Management Board, 11 October 1989, *Capacity Assurance Plan,* St. Paul, Minnesota.

45. Minnesota received a total of $56,744,749 in Superfund money from the EPA between 1983 and 1994 (Minnesota Office of Environmental Assistance 1994).

46. Memorandum, Jack Ditmore, Minnesota Environmental Quality Board, 10 April 1989, 3.
The WMB was temporarily placed under the jurisdiction of the Environmental Quality Board for about a year during a period of administrative reorganization.

47. Ibid.

48. Neil Miller, Public Affairs Officer, Waste Management Board, interview with author, St. Paul, Minnesota, 29 April 1990.

49. See Chapter 5 and Appendix C of Minnesota's *Capacity Assurance Plan* for further details.

50. Memorandum, Jack Ditmore, Minnesota Environmental Quality Board, 10 April 1989, 3.

51. It should be noted that county residents were reluctant to accept this provision. Some citizens believed that the facility would be useful for Minnesota and could therefore accept having it in their county, but it was harder to justify the facility in their community if it was serving out-of-state businesses. This issue is discussed in more detail in Chapter 4, where I explore the results from a citizen survey and interviews with state officials.

52. Memorandum, Terri Ann Port to Hazardous Waste Planning Council, "Summary of Issues Regarding Facility Development Program," 3 March 1989, 2.

53. Neil Miller, Public Affairs Officer, Waste Management Board, interview with author, St. Paul, Minnesota, 29 April 1990.

54. Terri Ann Port, Director of Facility Development, Minnesota Waste Management Board, quoted in the *Minneapolis Star and Tribune,* 26 March 1989, 1B.

55. Memorandum, Terri Ann Port to Hazardous Waste Planning Council, "Summary of Issues Regarding Facility Development Program," 3 March 1989, 5.

56. Joseph Pavelich, quoted in *Northome Record,* 10 May 1988, 10.

57. Ibid.

58. Neil Miller, Public Affairs Officer, Waste Management Board, interview with author, St. Paul, Minnesota, 29 April 1990.

59. Russ Susag, Environmental Officer 3M Corporation, interview with author, St. Paul, Minnesota, 30 June 1990.

60. The tipping fees for the proposed stabilization and containment facility were $330 per ton, according to the Waste Management Board's estimates in its *Stabilization and Containment Report* of 1988. At that time 3M was paying approximately $100 per ton to dispose of its incinerator ash in a landfill in Illinois.

61. Russ Susag, Environmental Officer 3M Corporation, interview with author, St. Paul, Minnesota, 30 June 1992.

62. Ibid.

63. The clay base keeps water near the surface. For hazardous waste sites, this adds a layer of protection, since a leak from a disposal facility cannot easily contaminate underground aquifers.

64. Letter from Dan Shuster to Senator Robert Lessard, 20 January 1989, Minnesota Historical Society, St. Paul, Minnesota.

65. Dan Shuster, President of Metropolitan Recovery Corporation, interviewed by Laurel Beager and Tom Klein in "MRS Sees State as Competition," *Daily Journal,* 1 March 1989, 1. Later MRS stated that it would be willing to use the containment part of the stabilization and containment facility.

66. Diane Jensen, Clean Water Action Committee, interview with author, Minneapolis, Minnesota, 25 July 1990; Bob Lowman, Preserve Our Land, telephone interview with author, 3 August 1990.

67. Memorandum, Terri Ann Port to Hazardous Waste Planning Council, "Summary of Issues Regarding Facility Development Program," 3 March 1989, 3.

68. Neil Miller, Public Affairs Officer, Waste Management Board, interview with author, St. Paul, Minnesota, 29 April 1990.

69. Ken Stabler, Acting Director of Facility Development, Waste Management Board, interview with author, Minneapolis, Minnesota, 20 June 1990.

Citizen preference for state ownership over private ownership is not necessarily inconsistent with the evidence from 1983, in which citizens opposed state development of a facility. In 1983 the issue was whether the state should take over the facility development if private-sector firms would not get involved. (In other words, should the state rescue the project?) In 1988 the state was already deeply involved in the process and the issue was its level of involvement.

70. In making these calculations of the profitability of the facility, state officials chose to set the return that the state got from the facility equal to the cost of the facility plus the interest on the debt that the state would incur. Thus they set the social discount rate between present and future consumption equal to market interest rates. In addition, they recognized that the state would have to subsidize the facility for the first few years but would get that money back over the lifetime of the facility from user fees. However, this

second set of calculations did not include a discount rate, thus implicitly suggesting that society had no preference between present and future consumption. Both of these decisions made it easier to claim that the facility would be profitable. (For details of their calculations, see Minnesota Waste Management Board, 1988, *Stabilization and Containment: Report on Facility Development,* St. Paul, Minnesota.)

71. Joseph Pavelich, quoted in "List of Counties in WMB Site Search Trimmed Down To Eight," *Red Lake Falls Gazette,* 25 November 1987, 1.

72. Federal regulations specify that producers of hazardous waste are responsible for any damages caused by the waste even after it has been disposed of. The state of Minnesota could not remove the liability since it is codified under federal law, but it could help pay insurance premiums or agree to insure the facility above the $40 million of coverage that the operator was required to purchase. The concerns of the environmental groups appeared to be well grounded since, in her progress report, Terri Port wrote, "3M's decision to use the facility probably would be based on cost and the level of indemnification from liability the state would provide." Memorandum, Terri Ann Port to Hazardous Waste Planning Council, "Summary of Issues Regarding Facility Development Program," 3 March 1989, 6.

# CHAPTER 3

# The Strategic State: Hazardous Waste Siting Through Inducements and Persuasion

There is a growing consensus among those who study hazardous waste siting that a successful siting strategy should include both citizens and experts in the decision-making process (for a review, see Munton 1996). This cooperative approach is endorsed partly because of the repeated failure of siting attempts, like the one first tried by Minnesota, in which states and municipalities draw on their powers of eminent domain to force communities to accept facilities. A siting strategy that includes citizen participation is also advocated because it will help ensure that the process will be fair and democratic.

It was partly with these goals in mind (successful siting and a fair and equitable process) that the state of Minnesota embarked on its voluntary siting process. Because strategies like the one Minnesota attempted are seen as promising, the lessons from that state are important. What is significant about Minnesota's experience is that a seemingly benign process was not perceived as fair by citizens who were supposed to benefit from it and the process was not effective, if effectiveness is measured by successful siting.

The voluntary part of Minnesota's siting process, which was initiated in 1986, marked an important change in the decision-making process. It was at this point that the conflict evolved into a struggle between technocrats and citizens. As the previous chapter demonstrated, the Waste Management Board, the agency charged with implementing the Waste Management Act, gained a high degree of autonomy after the failure of the first siting attempt through eminent domain. Its autonomy arose out of the breakdown of elite policy networks, the ensuing political stalemate between citizens and elite interest groups, and uncertainty within the legislature about how to proceed. Although business and environmental groups played an important role in the early stages of the process, the state was able to resist the pressures from key businesses to continue the search for a landfill close to the Twin Cities and opted instead for the stabilization and containment facility and volunteer siting process. Environmental groups as well opposed this solution, arguing that such a facility was no longer necessary, would be too expensive, and, most important, would create disincentives to waste reduction and recycling.

Despite this opposition, the Waste Management Board pushed ahead with the siting process, defending the facility as in the long-term interest of the state. State officials were guided in their decision-making by both institutional pressures and personal preferences. Federal regulations requiring states to develop a long-term plan to manage its hazardous waste and the moral commitment of state officials to ensuring that Minnesota dispose of its own waste both played a key role in the officials' decision to pursue a site.

However, according to state theorists, for state actors to bring their autonomously formed policy prescriptions to fruition, the state must develop capacity as well as autonomy. The development of state autonomy in the second phase of Minnesota's hazardous waste siting effort was not sufficient to ensure that state actors would have a direct and independent influence on policymaking; they also needed to obtain the *capacity* to implement their policy preferences, particularly if faced with strong opposition from citizens.

Within the state literature different types of state capacity are emphasized. In her rendering of state capacity, Skocpol argues that once the state has been shown to have autonomy, "one may then explore the 'capacities' of states to implement official goals, especially over the actual or potential opposition of powerful social economic circumstances" (Skocpol 1985, 9). Thus, in her understanding of state capacity, Skocpol focuses on the coercive capacity of the state (i.e., the ability of state actors to pursue their policies over societal opposition). The state's capacity to overcome opposition is dependent on the organizational characteristics of the state. State actors working within established organizations, developing a coherent mission, and having a high degree of expertise will be particularly effective in implementing their autonomous policy preferences (Skocpol and Finegold 1982).[1] These resources allow state actors to resist public opposition and to work systematically and authoritatively in pursuit of their policy preferences. On an issue like hazardous waste policy, the state's coercive capacity is of special significance because it can draw on its powers of eminent domain in making hazardous waste decisions as well as on its organizational strength.

Despite the usefulness of "coercive capacity" as a concept for describing activities undertaken by the state, the state has noncoercive powers that it can draw on as well. The state's noncoercive powers are particularly important in situations in which it is attempting to gain the consent of the governed rather than override their preferences. This alternative conception of state capacity as noncoercive is developed explicitly by state theorists like Nordlinger (1981), and implicitly by specialists in hazardous waste policy (Portney 1991; Elliot 1984). As Nordlinger argues in his notion of Type II Autonomy, state officials can use their resources to try to gain allies for their positions, to alter the nature of the debate, or to convince citizens of the merits of public officials' thinking.[2] Because of the state's internal resources (time, expertise, and money, to name a few), it does not have to take societal interests as fixed or simply rely on its superior political power to coerce consent. Rather, it can induce the cooperation of citizens or persuade citizens that the state's policy preferences are in their own best interest.[3] In Minnesota, the state relied on its financial and intellectual resources in an attempt to gain citizen acceptance of the proposed facility rather than exercising its powers of eminent domain.

Although the state's noncoercive powers have been given less attention than its coercive powers in academic research, it is of primary importance in understanding the making of public policy in a democratic state. As Lindblom suggests, "If control of the mind or coerced obedience in behavior stand as alternatives, democracy has chosen the former" (Lindblom 1990, 110).

Recent trends in policymaking provide evidence of the ability of the state to use its financial, intellectual, and technical resources to gain the consent of the governed. In particular, states attempting to site hazardous waste facilities have adopted compensation strategies as a means for inducing acceptance of hazardous waste facilities by the local communities (O'Hare, Bacow, and Sanderson 1983; Elliot 1984; Portney 1988, 1991; Frey and Oberholzer-Gee 1996; Frey, Oberholzer-Gee, and Eichenberger 1996; Inhaber 1998). At the same time that states have promised financial incentives they have marshaled their technical and scientific expertise in an attempt to persuade the public of the safety and wisdom of policies that they are pursuing. States also often attempt to structure decision-making in ways that they hope will lead to a favorable outcome. Thus state power is not limited to coercive capacity but includes the resources to persuade or induce support for its proposals as well.

This emphasis on the state's capacity and state actors' willingness to attempt to alter citizen preferences provides a different conceptualization of the policy process than the more general common view in which citizens exert pressure on policymakers. In his writing on the relationship between public opinion and public policy, Weissberg argues:

> [I]mplicit in most analyses of the relationship between public opinion and public policy is that if influence is exerted, it is exerted by citizens on political leaders. . . . Nevertheless, opinion-policy congruences can also be achieved through the reverse process: government influencing mass opinion. (Weissberg 1976, 222)[4]

As Weissberg suggests, most research in policymaking is grounded in a pluralist understanding of the political process, in which state actors respond to external pressures in making policy. The use of the state's noncoercive powers suggests the opposite, namely that state officials attempt to enact their policy preferences by altering the preferences of citizens who might rise in opposition to the policy they are pursuing.[5]

In this chapter I describe the actions taken by the state of Minnesota as it faced intense public opposition. Because of the state officials' commitment to this facility as the best long-term solution to Minnesota's hazardous waste problem, they used their institutional resources to try to gain the consent of citizens for the facility. The strategy can be divided into two parts: (1) the state's use of financial compensation and attempts to alter the decision-making structure to gain an advantage and (2) its more overt attempts at managing public opinion. This chapter will demonstrate the Waste Management Board's reliance on these inducements after its attempt to site a hazardous waste facility through eminent domain failed and will illustrate the importance of the state's noncoercive powers as it attempted to gain consent from its citizens. In addition, it will help show that the relationship between state actors' preferences and citizens' preferences is not fixed since the state can use its resources to try to alter citizens' preferences. Finally, it will show the possibilities for political control of the administrative state given its potential for developing autonomy and capacity.

## The Structure of Decision-Making

Because decision-making authority rested with the state, state officials could restructure the process in ways that they felt would facilitate successful siting. After the failure of the eminent domain siting in 1984, these officials reevaluated the siting project and devised a plan they hoped would be more successful. The most important change in Minnesota's decision-making structure for hazardous waste policy was the move from an eminent domain program to one of voluntary siting. The WMB was convinced that a voluntary program would allow the state to secure a site and overcome the public opposition that had plagued the first phase of the siting project. Early in the siting process Brett Smith of the WMB staff promised "that the Board will do an aggressive search to find a volunteer and believes it can succeed."[6]

### Overview of the Voluntary Process

The siting program was revamped by the WMB and approved by the state legislature in the 1986 Amendments to the Waste Management Act. The new program allowed counties to volunteer as candidates for the stabilization and containment facility. For a county to volunteer, a majority of the county board had to agreed to send a nonbinding Resolution of Interest to the Waste Management Board. The WMB would evaluate sites within each of the volunteer counties based on geological criteria, while the county would evaluate the risks and benefits of the facility to them. The counties that made it through the preliminary phase of the site selection process would be invited to negotiate a contract with the state, detailing the terms and conditions under which they would accept the facility.

Volunteer counties were provided with monthly payments in exchange for their participation in the siting process. The money was justified as a way for the counties to study the risks and benefits that the facility might provide for their county as well as to assess the support for the facility among county residents. Counties received this money as long as they remained on the state's list of potential hosts of the facility. Therefore the longer the county stayed with the process, the more money it would receive from the state.

Originally counties received $4,000 per month, but this was later raised to $6,000. Although the money was budgeted by the state to be used for studying the local impact of the facility, it was placed in the county's general revenue fund and each county could decide how the money should be allocated and what amount, if any, was to be used to study the facility.

In addition, each volunteer county was required to convene an advisory council made up of its citizens. County boards were allowed to select members of the council based on their own criteria. The advisory councils were designed to assess the benefits and risks that the facility would bring to the county and help determine the level of support for the facility among county residents. The councils were asked to make a recommendation to the county board once their investigations were complete. The county boards retained final authority to determine whether to proceed to the second phase of the process, which was to negotiate a contract with the state.

The terms that could be included in the contract were not specified in the 1986 Amendments to the Waste Management Act. The WMB was authorized to negotiate a contract for the state which would then be subject to legislative approval. The WMB maintained close contact with the LCWM to ensure some correspondence between what the legislature might approve and what the WMB would negotiate. However, because of the lack of specificity, nothing was certain about a contract until the legislature approved it.

Background to the Counties

Given the general reluctance of communities to consent to the construction of a hazardous waste facility near them, the most obvious question that emerges from this case study of Minnesota's hazardous waste policy is why counties would volunteer to be a site for a hazardous waste facility. One explanation points to the demographic and economic conditions of a host community as the key to whether a facility will be accepted. A 1984 report prepared by a consulting firm for the California Waste Management Board gave the following recommendations:

The communities least resistant include: 1) rural 2) low income 3) jobless (especially if new jobs are promised) 4) communities with free-market conservative attitudes 5) elderly populations 6) a majority of long-time residents and 7) low education. In general, those areas where farming and ranching represent the base economy are the most desirable to be considered for various dump sites.[7]

The communities with the most extensive involvement with the proposed facility in Minnesota were two rural counties, Red Lake and Koochiching. Both counties are in the northern part of the state and are approximately 250 miles from the Minneapolis-St. Paul metropolitan area, the source of most of the state's hazardous waste. Both counties are sparsely populated, relative to the rest of Minnesota's counties. (According to the 1980 census, Koochiching is ranked 48th [16,299 residents] and Red Lake is 81st [4,525 residents] in population, out of eighty-four Minnesota counties.) Each county has an aging population, which is only exacerbated by the poor economic conditions that force many of the younger county residents to leave the area in pursuit of employment. In the late 1980s both counties were struggling economically, with unemployment between 10 and 20 percent in Red Lake during the winter months. (Additional demographic information on the counties is provided in Appendix A.)

Neither county has a particularly strong industrial base, and therefore local industry would not be directly utilizing the facility. The only significant industrial production in Koochiching County is in the town of International Falls, where a Boise Cascade paper mill operates. It is the largest industrial producer and employer in the county. A related industry in the county is logging, the principle supplier of raw material to the paper plant. The other important source of revenue for citizens in the county is tourism. Voyager National Park is located in the county and is a heavily used recreational area in the summer months. In addition, the Rainy River is a popular boating and fishing area.

Red Lake County, on the other hand, survives primarily on agricultural production. Most of the acreage in the county is devoted to farming. There is some retail business in the county seat, Red Lake Falls, but because of its proximity to larger cities in adjacent counties, local retailers must compete with bigger department stores and chain stores.

Although citizens in both counties mounted significant opposition campaigns, it is not surprising that these counties were the ones most interested in housing a hazardous waste facility. Supporters of the facility in the counties saw it as an opportunity to bring the counties out of their economic malaise. County commissioners in both counties recognized the need for new jobs in their area to revitalize their flagging economies. Don Sandbeck,

Koochiching County commissioner, argued that the town of Northome, in particular, sought the facility to strengthen its weak economy. "The southern part of the county [the Northome area] is kind of a dying area where the economy is really down, there is nothing there. People were moving and all you've got were older senior citizens."[8] The county commissioners realized that although the facility itself would bring new jobs to the county, some of these jobs would be highly specialized and it was unlikely that these skills could be found within the county. As a result, most of the jobs that county residents might have qualified for would have been in maintenance and trucking.

More important for county officials was the compensation package from the state. According to the 1986 Amendments to the Minnesota Waste Management Act, the counties would negotiate the terms under which they would accept the facility with the Waste Management Board. The counties could seek economic development funds, property tax relief for county residents, additional funding for schools and transportation, and a host of other benefits.

One proposal was to use the money from the state as seed money to stimulate new business growth in the county:

> I would hope that the county could use the money to provide some economic development that would be really beneficial to the county. If you have 5 to 10 million dollars in a bank, you can build a plant. Rather than saying [to a prospective developer] that we can provide you a tax-free deal, we can help finance development.[9]

Some of the citizens on the advisory committee looking into the feasibility of the facility echoed these sentiments. They saw the facility as a way to boost their economy and preserve their communities.[10]

In both counties grassroots opposition groups organized and were quite active in the campaign to keep the facility out of their county. The Koochiching organization was called the Northland Concerned Citizens (NCC). These citizens consistently challenged the claims made by the state about safety and the need for the facility, tried to pressure the state into funding independent experts to speak to citizens about the facility, used the media to try to persuade other residents of the illegitimacy of the program, and applied constant pressure to county commissioners to withdraw from the siting process. In addition, because this was a grassroots organization that financed its operations through fundraisers like the sale of cookbooks, the state created a public relations problem for itself since it looked like a well-financed lobbyist in comparison to these homespun organizations.

In Koochiching an organization also arose in support of the facility. This organization, Concerned Citizens for a Clean Environment, surfaced late in the process and argued that "there was a large segment of the population that probably didn't agree with NCC, but were reticent to voice it and so we're just a bunch of people that feel a need to put some positive emphasis on what we feel are the benefits of a facility like this."[11] Among the benefits that they emphasized were the need to cope with the problems of an industrialized society and to provide safe storage of the waste by-products.

In Red Lake County only one group, the Concerned Citizens Against Hazardous Waste, formed and was opposed to the hazardous waste facility. This organization employed tactics similar to those of the Northland Concerned Citizens. In fact the two organizations exchanged information and provided support to each other while both counties were still candidates. The Concerned Citizens Against Hazardous Waste sent representatives to most county meetings, used the media to broadcast their opposition, and, like their counterpart in Koochiching, financed their operations through bake sales.

These groups used a variety of sources and strategies to gather and disseminate information. The opposition groups independently checked the performance of facilities managed by International Technologies (IT), the company hired to develop and run the state's facility. These citizens culled newspapers and periodicals and found that the company had been fined $3.2 million for violations in California and $375,000 for violations of the State Code of Ethics in Louisiana.[12] These fines and what they suggested about the safety of the facility became a key issue in the public debate. Citizens also contacted the mayor of Benicia, the city in which IT's California facility was located, to find out more about its operations. They studied watershed maps to assess how close the proposed sites were to communities and where contaminated water would flow should a leak or spill occur. In Koochiching County citizens researched the amount of waste that was produced in their county and learned that it was only 1 percent of the state's total. This raised questions of fairness, since many wondered why a county with so little waste should bear most of the risk associated with the disposal of hazardous materials.

Citizens in these groups also contributed to the debate about this issue by reading reports and information provided by the WMB about the facility, and they challenged some of the state's interpretations of this information. For example, using the WMB's estimates of the amount of waste produced in the state and the price that it could charge for its disposal, citizens questioned whether the facility would really be economically viable without bringing waste in from other states. They also contested the WMB's claim that the facility would provide a boost for the local economy and employment opportunities for local residents. The WMB's own report showed that the facility would employ only twenty-four to thirty-one workers, many of whom would have to be brought in from outside the county.[13]

In both counties the opposition groups and the group that supported the facility used the local newspapers as a way to disseminate information to other citizens. The *Northome Record* and the *International Falls Journal* in Koochiching County and the *Red Lake Falls Gazette* used their Letters to the Editor sections as a forum for communication on this issue. In each county supporters and opponents of the facility, as well as the WMB, participated in lengthy and ongoing debates in these papers about the safety of and need for the facility. In addition, opponents in each county bought advertising space in these newspapers to counter the advertisements purchased by the WMB to promote the facility.

The Exercise of Noncoercive Capacity

Despite the latitude the WMB enjoyed in designing and pursuing its vision of a hazardous waste policy for Minnesota, it had only weak capacity because legislators were reluctant to grant the state's power of eminent domain a second time and risk further outrage from their constituents. Successful siting was thus dependent on the ability of the WMB to gain citizen cooperation in the siting process. Counties that volunteered would be offered compensation to accept the facility, and at the same time the WMB would use its technical expertise to convince citizens of the importance and safety of the facility. Though the state lacked the coercive capacity to force citizens to cooperate, it did have important technical and financial resources to win their cooperation.

The voluntary process was designed to overcome earlier resistance to a hazardous waste facility sited through eminent domain.[14] It gave the state several advantages that might ensure success. First, the voluntary process provided a way to identify counties where the WMB would be welcome, at least by a number of "respected leaders" like county board members.

> Since the county has expressed an interest in the process, there are usually several key people in the county who are in favor of the review process. By having recognizable and respectable leaders involved in the review process, trust and credibility are greatly enhanced.[15]

Under the eminent domain strategy, the state would pick a site based on geological characteristics and use its coercive powers to implement the choice, despite public opposition. The voluntary process, however, produced candidate counties that were at least somewhat sympathetic to the process from the beginning, otherwise they would not have volunteered.

Likewise, with the county board and advisory committees at the center of the local process, the WMB hoped to maintain a low public profile and avoid being seen as outsiders trying to foist the facility on an unwilling community. The WMB recognized that "it is important to note that the study area selection process is led by the local citizen committee, with the WMB providing technical assistance and guidance when it is requested."[16] Local control was central to the entire siting process, since counties entered the process by volunteering, and the final decision to withdraw a county from consideration or to accept the facility rested with that county's board.

Because there were no specific guidelines for contract negotiations, the WMB took an open-ended approach in negotiations with the state's counties. Prior to the negotiations WMB representatives encouraged county negotiating teams to think broadly about what they wanted in exchange for accepting the site and to include these items in their list of issues to negotiate. Negotiators for both the state and the county referred to these demands as the "wish list." Included in the Koochiching County "wish list," for example, were requests for 100 percent residential tax credit for its homestead owners, a 100 percent tax credit for businesses located within 15 miles of the site, capital funding and technical assistance for the development of a solid waste facility in the county, and education or reeducation for local residents desiring employment at the facility. In Red Lake County the contract negotiated with the state included payments to the county of $24 million over twenty-three years, as well as a property value assurance program for homeowners in the county and financial assistance to qualified county residents for technical and vocational training.[17] This open-ended approach to negotiations enabled the state to adapt the facility and the terms of the contract to match local concerns, thereby encouraging counties to participate and allowing them to explore possible benefits.

The ambiguity associated with contract negotiations left the WMB with additional rules to settle in negotiations. The WMB attempted to get the information exchanged with the county representatives classified as "non-public." According to the WMB, this information contained trade secrets and financial data that should not be released because they would hurt the competitive position of the companies selected to build and manage the facility. The WMB felt that this privacy would also work to the advantage of the counties since they could keep their bids from being scrutinized by one another. However, it could also benefit the state because ignorance of what other counties bid might drive down the price a county would ask.

To abide by Minnesota's Data Privacy Act, the WMB had to submit its request for classifying the information to the state's Administrative Commissioner, Sandra J. Hale. She approved part of the WMB's request, allowing data that the WMB was using to negotiate with the counties to be classified. However, she refused to classify correspondence and information passed from the county to the WMB, and thus much of the information remained public.[18]

As this section shows, in Minnesota the public officials attempted to use their institutional resources to structure the decision-making process to gain consent for the facility. With the voluntary process the receptive communities would sign on as potential candidates for the hazardous waste site rather than have the WMB wrestle consent from an unwilling community. The voluntary process would provide modest compensation to those counties that volunteered, and it promised more substantial payments to the county that was eventually chosen. In addition, the WMB members tried to use their knowledge of state laws to minimize public scrutiny of the contract until private negotiations with the chosen county were completed.


## Managing Public Opinion

Because of the resources at the disposal of state personnel, the WMB could develop and implement strategies to manage public opinion. These included running an education campaign to develop citizen understanding of the hazardous waste problem and the solutions the facility promised, organizing a media relations campaign to gain favorable press coverage, staffing an informational office at the time of a proposed referendum in Koochiching County, and making moral arguments about the need for the facility as a long-term benefit to Minnesota.

Educating the Public

Of central importance to the WMB's plan to site a hazardous waste facility in Minnesota was the implementation of a thorough public education campaign to convince residents in the volunteer counties of the benefits and safety of the stabilization and containment facility.[19] State officials were hopeful that if citizens were aware of the same facts as state officials, they would see the economic benefits of the facility to the surrounding community as well as the environmental and economic benefits to the state as a whole.

To educate the communities involved in the process, the state held informational meetings in homes and for groups in the volunteer counties. At these meetings they presented information about the type of waste to be stored in the facility, the design of the plant, and the safety features it included. As part of the demonstration the WMB brought a sample of the hazardous waste to be stored in the facility and allowed county residents to touch it. (According to the Waste Management Board, because the waste products are primarily heavy metals like lead, chromium, and cadmium, they are not a threat to humans unless ingested. The primary threat to humans is through leaching into the groundwater and thereby contaminating the drinking water [Dames and Moore 1990].) The Waste Management Board preferred to conduct these informational meetings in small, informal settings rather than in large, formal meetings.

The WMB also conducted a number of conferences on hazardous waste issues in rural Minnesota for county commissioners and others involved in the siting process. These seminars were justified as a way of gaining consent for the facility.

Under the same philosophy applied in educating its clientele directly, the board sought the assistance of influential members of environmental groups and gave them the opportunity to understand the issues and processes. Gaining their support would mitigate the highly-charged political controversy associated with programs, ultimately reducing the level of effort and expense needed to progress programs to their successful conclusions.[20]

In addition, the WMB contracted with a sociologist and private consultant who specialized in helping site facilities. Dr. Jennifer McQuaid-Cook
advised the Waste Management Board on a number of issues relating to
siting. She had assisted in the siting of a facility similar to the one proposed
in Minnesota that had been built in Swan Hills, Alberta, Canada. As part of
her consulting fee she helped arrange tours of the Swan Hills facility and
meetings with Swan Hills officials, and answered questions from individuals
who toured the facility. McQuaid-Cook also helped the WMB

> evaluate the technical siting criteria to be used by the Environmental
> Quality Board (EQB) to determine the physical, biological, and social
> suitability of an area, and to provide feedback, guidance, and recom-
> mendations on the public information program developed by the
> EQB.[21]

In 1987 members of the Koochiching County Advisory Council, along
with advisory council members from other counties, toured the Swan Hills
facility. They saw how the waste was transported to the facility, how it was
processed, and how safety features in the transportation and processing of
the waste were designed to minimize the threat of contamination to the local
environment. In addition, the delegation met with citizens and community
leaders to discuss the social and economic impact of the facility on the
community. Although the facility had only been in operation for two weeks
at the time of the visit, Swan Hills residents were optimistic that their facility
would be an economic boon to the community and would help it overcome
the economic hardships it faced with the decline of the oil industry in the
area.[22] However, some Minnesota residents who were opposed to their own
facility saw this visit to the Swan Hills facility as an attempt to mislead
citizens since it had just opened. They argued that the delegation should
have been sent to an older facility that was experiencing difficulty meeting
environmental regulations to see the other side of waste disposal.[23]

Managing Media Relations

One of the most important components of the state's management of public
opinion was its attention to and use of the media. The WMB hired outside
consultants to help develop a plan for working with the print, radio, and
television media in the volunteer counties. For example, Media Rare, a

consulting group, had a contract for $29,000 to develop a strategy for working with the media.

The board's March 1987 supplemental agreement with Media Rare, Inc. requires the consultant to "assist Waste Management Board staff in communicating and coordinating volunteer program activities with the media, organizations, and all other clientele interested in or affected by Waste Management Board stabilization and containment programs."[24]

In addition, in January 1988 the WMB signed a contract with Mona, Meyer and McGrath for $10,000 to help develop a comprehensive mission statement for use in communication planning and to draft "an overall communication plan . . . and an implementation plan for the ensuing twelve months."[25]

As part of its plan to help ensure that the stabilization and containment facility would receive favorable publicity in the volunteer counties, WMB personnel held weekly meetings with media representatives.[26] In these meetings they provided information packets about the stabilization and containment facility and illustrations and photographs of it for the local media.

The WMB also monitored the stories that were published in the newspapers or aired on the television and radio stations that served the counties. When unfavorable information was presented by the media, the WMB would, at times, take steps to protect against additional negative information being released in the future. In reporting to the Waste Management Board about media activities around Red Lake County, Terri Port, the WMB's Director of Facility Development, stated that the first "completely negative article" regarding the facility was published by the *Grand Forks Herald* and picked up by the AP wire. "She stated that she asked Steve Weiss, the author of the article, to verify his information in the future with the WMB staff before going to print."[27]

The WMB also contracted with a newspaper clipping service to collect articles related to the stabilization and containment facility that appeared in local newspapers. Often when information in these papers was thought to make erroneous claims a member of the WMB would write a letter correcting the comments made by reporters, editors, or readers (in the newspapers' Letters to the Editor). For example, Joseph Pavelich, one of the chairs of the Waste Management Board, wrote a letter to the editor of the *Littlefork Times* taking issue with the claims made in an editorial by Kathleen McQuillan, an editor of the paper. He challenged her assertions that the WMB was pressuring the counties to accept the facility, even though it was, in his words, "stepping up its informational campaign." He went on to correct her statement that waste incineration would be involved in the hazardous waste facility that was being proposed in Koochiching County. These corrective actions taken by the WMB provide testimony to its commitment to manage and monitor the information presented to residents in candidate counties.

According to Pavelich, the expenditures for consultants to help develop plans to guide the WMB's relations with the media were necessary to the successful siting of a hazardous waste facility. "A thorough, well-developed public information program," Pavelich argued, "would be essential to the success of the board's controversial and highly charged political programs. It was necessary to contract for professional public affairs advice because the expertise was not available from the board at the time."[28]

Public relations and media relations are an important part of the state's noncoercive powers in its efforts to gain the consent of the governed for its programs. Page and Shapiro (1992, Chapter 9) argue that on issues for which the public has limited information, like foreign policy, overt attempts at manipulation do occur. They note the misleading reports about the Gulf of Tonkin incident by the Johnson administration to gain support for additional involvement in Vietnam and the gross inflation of the missile capability of the Soviet Union by the Kennedy administration to increase military funding. On domestic policy matters they argue that the public was misled by both Lyndon Johnson's attempt to "oversell" the war on poverty through low cost estimates and Richard Nixon's efforts to discredit the program by overstating the shortcomings of the Great Society programs.

Weissberg (1976) notes that many of these efforts to gain public approval of government programs are undertaken indirectly by providing the media with news releases, films, and even complete news "stories." In addition, Page and Shapiro (1992) describe the ways in which the media cooperate with those in power by not raising questions about how the economic system in the United States is organized. In their study of political knowledge, Delli-Carpini and Keeter (1996) argue that the media's coverage of events like the Gulf War help shape opinions and knowledge about a problem so that they are aligned with the administration's position (99–100). (See also

Page's *Who Deliberates*, 1996.) Thus Minnesota's experience, as Robert Weissberg observes, is not an isolated one:

> Though one may associate "public relations" with the activities of big business concerned about their public image, the United States government wages perhaps the largest PR program in the world. . . . [E]ven the most conservative estimates show that hundreds of millions of dollars each year are spent publicizing the activities and accomplishments of government to its own citizens.[29]

## Information Office

One of the more controversial decisions made by the WMB as part of its public relations campaign was to establish an information office in Koochiching County at the time of a proposed referendum (although the referendum never took place). The office was scheduled to open on 14 August, approximately one month prior to the proposed referendum, and closed 13 September, one day after it. The WMB felt that "this office would provide a needed WMB presence in the community prior to a public referendum on the social acceptability of locating a stabilization and containment facility in the Northome area."[30]

The office was to be staffed full-time by a local resident and part-time by WMB staff and would serve as a source of information to residents prior to the referendum. Many residents, however, perceived the WMB's actions as staging a campaign operation to win support for the facility in the referendum, rather than simply as staffing an informational office.[31] This action by the WMB fueled suspicions among some county residents that the WMB was trying to "sell" the facility to the county.[32] Bruce Biggins, the Koochiching County commissioner opposed to the facility, argued, "this clearly is a campaign office intended to influence the outcome of the election."[33]

## Moral Suasion

One of the less overt but important tactics used by the Waste Management Board to gain consent for the facility was moral suasion. Because they believed that this facility would serve the long-term interests of the state by providing safe disposal of hazardous waste, the WMB tried to use moral arguments to persuade county residents to accept the facility. They tried to convince county residents who opposed it that they were acting narrowly and subverting the general welfare of the state. Accusations that opponents were victims of the Nimby syndrome were frequently leveled. In response to the withdrawal of two counties (Martin and Norman) from the siting effort because of public opposition, Joseph Pavelich, Chair of the Waste Management Board, wrote,

> The withdrawal of Martin and Norman counties illustrates the need for an increased level of public understanding about waste issues. We are increasing our public education efforts to overcome misconceptions about the facility, but for many people it's still very easy to say "not in my backyard," instead of learning about the issue and working with us toward a solution.[34]

Susan Boyle, a member of the Koochiching County advisory committee and an opponent of the facility, charged that the WMB personnel tried to "guilt them into accepting the facility" by arguing that it was in Minnesota's best interest and that blocking the development of the facility would jeopardize the environment in the future.[35]

Claims by state officials that they are looking out for the general welfare can serve as an important tool in land-use debates. Opponents are frequently charged with parochialism when they resist state plans to site a facility that imposes costs on a specific community and may benefit the general population. The danger of these arguments in the hands of public officials is that they can use these claims of the Nimby syndrome to rebut opponents and cast them as obstructionists rather than focusing the debate on the need for and safety of such a facility.

There is little sensitivity among state officials to the fact that there are both good and bad siting attempts. The Nimby syndrome becomes a self-confirming argument by state officials, since anyone who opposes facilities with some potential risk to surrounding communities can be accused of being victims of the Nimby syndrome. The power of this language accrues to state officials who are deemed to be working in "the general interest."[36]

All of these activities undertaken by the WMB—planning an information office, hiring consultants, working with the local media, and taking the moral high ground—demonstrate the advantages that the state has over citizens in the county in getting its message across. The Waste Management Board and the legislature used state revenues to devise and carry out a plan to persuade residents of the safety and benefits of this facility, but county residents who opposed the facility had to rely on their own resources to struggle against the state. During the siting effort in Koochiching County, residents challenged the state's use of tax revenues to launch this information campaign. At one point, the state was asked by Jody Gross, an opponent of the facility, to account for the amount of money that it had spent on siting the facility. In Koochiching the state spent an estimated $90,000 in salaries and travel expenses from January 1987 through October 1988. In addition, the state paid consultant's fees to various media relations firms, as well as $35,000 to Dr. McQuaid-Cook, bringing the total to well over $100,000.[37] This does not include the money spent to send the advisory committee to Swan Hills, Alberta, to visit the hazardous waste facility there.

Such expenditures in Koochiching County as well as in other counties were justified by the WMB as necessary to gain support for this facility.

> The potential for success of the board's controversial programs, and even its popular programs, was greatly enhanced by choosing to meet our clientele in their home areas. This fostered good communication and trust. Funds disbursed for such activities were well invested.[38]

In contrast, the residents of the county opposed to the facility financed their campaign through money raised from bake sales, cookbook sales, and donations from citizens. They used the money to publicize information they felt would challenge the WMB's claims. In addition, they used their funds to bring in a speaker to present an alternative perspective on the facility from that offered by the Waste Management Board.

The funds given to the county in exchange for being a volunteer could have been used to pay for outside information, but the Koochiching County commissioners would not authorize funds for opposing views. Red Lake County was one of the few counties to allocate some of its monthly payments for an independent evaluation of the facility and the siting process. It hired an engineering firm, Dames and Moore, to study the WMB's plans and to examine them in light of the demographic and geological characteristics of Red Lake County.

In general, the state's efforts to gain the consent of a community focused on what state officials called "educating the public." The state did, however, consider at least one attempt to manipulate the public directly. An internal memorandum of the WMB described a discussion between legislators from Koochiching County and the WMB in which they contemplated a mailing to county residents just prior to the referendum to convince them of the merits of the project. Tom Johnson of the WMB reported in the memorandum that the legislators recommended

> an intensive public relations campaign. Their feeling was that all the residents would likely get the message this way without the tension of hearing the message in a controversial meeting setting. This would bring them to the polls with a better attitude toward being supportive. It also doesn't give the opposition an opportunity to rebut since the information and coverage would be distributed just ahead of the primary election.[39]

The exposure of this attempt at manipulation in the local media made it difficult for the WMB to overcome the sense that it was trying to sell the facility to a generally uninterested community. Many in the county came to view the WMB as "an agitator in our midst."[40]

## Demise of the Siting Process

Despite state officials' resolve to build a stabilization and containment facility and the advantages that the state held over opposition groups, they failed to site a facility in Minnesota using either eminent domain or a voluntary process. Eminent domain failed when citizens in the selected counties convinced their legislators to rethink the need for landfill disposal in Minnesota. It is more difficult to pinpoint a specific cause for the failure of the voluntary process since there were a number of problems associated with the design and implementation of it.

One of the potential pitfalls of the voluntary process that concerned the WMB from the beginning was the need for and difficulty of establishing trust. One member of the WMB argued, "Once a level of trust is established, effective technical risk discussions can begin. Until that level of trust has been established, risk communications may only be seen as part of a slick sales presentation" (Reinke 1988, 8).

As the interview materials and survey results indicate (presented more fully in Chapter 4), the Waste Management Board was never able to overcome citizens' suspicions that the facility was a great risk to county residents, nor were they able to convince them of the need for the facility.

Minnesota's experience with voluntary siting and economic incentives mirrors similar efforts across the country. In his in-depth study of Massachusetts's siting effort, Portney (1991) argues that economic inducements were ineffective in overcoming citizens' concerns about risk (see also O'Hare 1977; Morell and Magorian 1982; Frey, Oberholzer-Gee, and Eichenberger 1996).[41]

Despite the fact that the WMB recognized the need to establish trust, few of the activities in which they engaged in Red Lake and Koochiching Counties built residents' trust. For example, the rationale for the advisory committees was to institutionalize citizen involvement in the process and thus to legitimize the process and secure trust in the WMB. However, it appeared that the committees did not ultimately serve these ends. Many citizens within the county were suspicious of the advisory committee's ability to make an independent judgment. Part of this suspicion stemmed from the fact that the county commissioners, a majority of whom were interested in the facility, selected the committee members in the county. In addition, there were concerns that the advisory committees worked too closely with the WMB and relied too heavily on it for information about the facility.

> The committee members seem to truly want to do something for economic development but being brainwashed by the Waste Management Board is not the way. They have been wined and dined and taken to Edmonton to look at the facility there, but have any of them gone to an outside source to get another opinion on this issue?[42]

Ironically, the state's move from eminent domain to the voluntary process eroded trust by undermining state officials' claims of technical expertise. Under eminent domain the state was going to select "the best site," based upon its technical evaluation of geological characteristics like the proximity of underground aquifers, the soil characteristics of the site, and its impact on other local land uses. With the voluntary process the state could no longer defend a rural site as technically the best site. Therefore when rural residents asked, "Why is this facility not being built in the Twin Cities if it is so safe?" state officials could only say that the urban counties had not volunteered—not that these rural sites would provide greater safety due to geological characteristics.[43] This fed suspicions in the rural counties that the urban communities wanted to use these remote areas as their dumping grounds.

> We in northwestern Minnesota produce less than 1% of the hazardous waste in Minnesota, but they (Twin Cities public officials and residents) want us to store 99% of the hazardous waste from the whole state; 75% from the Twin Cities alone. Red Lake County, the smallest in Minnesota, is being considered for the waste dump.[44]

The voluntary process was further plagued by the ambiguities in the negotiation of a final contract between the county and the state as well as by uncertainty about the process by which final agreement would be reached. First, the Waste Management Board only served as a proxy, since the final contract was subject to final authorization by the full legislature. Therefore, throughout the negotiations both WMB and county negotiators were left guessing about the level of funding that the legislature would approve.

Second, the conditions under which the negotiations were to take place were never specified. In Koochiching County negotiators for the county wanted to close the negotiation meetings to the public. They wanted to "keep politics out of the negotiations."[45] Opponents of the facility saw this attempt to close the meetings as evidence that the WMB and the county negotiators were operating in an underhanded way. They believed that the meetings should be open so that public input could be made along the way, rather than citizens simply being forced to approve or disapprove the plan after it had been negotiated. In addition, citizens were skeptical that the county negotiating team was acting in the best interest of the county and felt that the team was being manipulated by the state negotiators and the county commissioners.[46]

Finally, there was uncertainty about the decision-making process itself. There were plans to hold a referendum to decide whether the facility would be sited in Koochiching County. However, Minnesota law precludes counties from conducting their own referenda without legislative approval. The first referendum proposed in the county had to be canceled because legislative approval had not been sought in advance.

This ambiguity was instrumental in that county's withdrawal from the siting process. Koochiching County had negotiated a contract of approximately $70 million in compensation with the negotiating team of the WMB.

Rather than send this contract to the legislature for immediate consideration, the Waste Management Board members decided to wait until they had negotiated a contract with Red Lake County, hoping that they might get a lower final price. There were also reports in the local papers that the WMB was beginning to have some doubts about the feasibility of and the need for the facility. Because of the turmoil the facility caused in Koochiching County and the feelings that the county was not being treated fairly by the state in the negotiations, county officials were not willing to sit and wait for the WMB to decide whether the contract was the best they could get. Therefore, immediately after the WMB's decision to wait on the contract the Koochiching County commissioners voted to withdraw the county as a candidate and put this issue behind them.

In Red Lake County the legislature did authorize a county-wide referendum on the issue. The debate over the issue grew quite intense as the WMB, citizens in the community supporting the facility, and opponents of the facility tried to get their message to the citizens of the county. According to provisions in the contract, the county would receive $24 million in monetary compensation from the state. It would also receive a share of any net profits that the facility produced during its twenty years of operation. County residents were promised a property value assurance program that would protect them from any losses in property value from the siting of the facility and financial assistance to those qualified for training to enable them to work in the facility.

The referendum was held on 6 November 1990. Despite all that they were offered, the county residents voted down the contract, 65 percent opposed to hosting the facility and 35 percent approving. The reasons for the opposition included a sense that the facility did not fit with their agricultural community, that Red Lake County was bearing the risks of a manufacturing economy with few of its benefits, and that the facility was not really necessary for Minnesota. The nature of the opposition is discussed in more detail in Chapter 4.

## Conclusion

The attempt by the state of Minnesota to site its stabilization and containment facility through a voluntary process demonstrates the important noncoercive resources that the state has at its disposal. The state can use these resources to pursue policies that do not have widespread support among societal groups, either established interest groups or unaffiliated citizens.

In this case citizens were subject to a variety of pressures from the state. The state's education campaign may be seen as an attempt to elevate the level of debate and improve democratic decision-making, but the disparity in resources between citizens and the state, and the fact that the agency seeking to find a site was also providing information as to its safety, made the education effort suspect in the minds of some citizens. In addition, the state tried to induce consent by promising financial compensation and by using moral suasion to convince citizens that opposition to the facility was inimical to the general welfare. The state's efforts to motivate support for its programs challenge conventional pluralist understandings of policymaking which emphasize the impact that citizens have on policymakers rather than the effect that public officials have on citizens (Truman 1951).

This case study demonstrates a more general point made by state theorists, namely, that the ability of state officials to gain autonomy and capacity has important consequences for the making of public policy. This case shows in particular that state capacity can take different forms as states draw on their coercive and noncoercive powers in an effort to implement policy prescriptions. State officials do not take societal preferences as fixed but instead attempt to alter them to coincide with their own preferences.

Yet Minnesota's hazardous waste siting effort from 1980 to 1990 also shows that despite important powers the state can be controlled by citizens. This finding challenges the claims of Lowi, Lindbolm, and state theorists who see citizens as having little or no input in the policymaking process.[47]

But state theorists' distinctions between autonomy and capacity can serve as a conceptual tool to identify how and where citizens insert themselves into the policymaking process. Because they faced different forms of state capacity in the first and second siting attempts, citizens were forced to adopt varying strategies to challenge the state's efforts. In the first phase citizen opposition was successful in disrupting elite decision-making by drawing the attention of legislators to the state's plans and to the impact that they would have on the community in which a landfill was sited. They raised doubts in the minds of their legislators as to the need for this facility in Minnesota. As a result, citizens held an implicit veto over the second phase of the siting effort because they, in conjunction with their county commissioners, could choose whether they wanted to accept the terms and conditions the state was offering. Those who opposed the stabilization and containment facility in these counties challenged the state's attempt to manage public opinion by drawing on independent sources of information and mobilizing their fellow citizens.

The ability of citizens to curtail the state's capacity when faced with both its coercive and noncoercive powers demonstrates that citizens hold some measure of political control over the state's administrative capacity. But the political control of citizens is limited in important ways. Even though citizens were able to block state initiatives and create a stalemate, they had little impact on the ability of the state to develop its autonomy and pursue plans to which citizens were opposed. More important, as the policy process unfolded in Minnesota citizens had few opportunities to redirect or restructure the way that the state would address the problem in the future.

However, this analysis raises questions about the appropriate role for citizens in the policy process. If citizen input continually results in deadlock or the inability of the state to act, what is a democratic state to do? Some policy experts take the technocratic view and argue that on complex issues like the siting of hazardous waste sites citizens should play a very limited role in the process and experts should be left to make the final decisions about such policies. According to this view, citizen input only obstructs the collective good by allowing parochial and naïve demands to filter into the decision-making process (Inhaber 1998; Ophuls 1977, 1992).

This perspective on citizen involvement is challenged by those with a more sanguine view regarding the role that citizens can and should play in the process (e.g., Dahl 1989; Lindblom 1990; Kraft and Clary 1991; Barber 1984; Fishkin 1995; on hazardous waste, see especially Williams and Matheny [1995] and Press [1994]). These scholars argue that policy decisions like the siting of hazardous waste facilities are fraught with value judgments, and that citizens working within the political process, rather than insulated policy experts, should be making these judgments.

The following chapter will develop these two perspectives on democratic decision-making and examine the debate by comparing citizens' and state officials' understandings of the risks and trade-offs that should be made in siting a hazardous waste facility. This more detailed analysis of citizens' and experts' thinking on hazardous waste policy will provide a better understanding of why deadlock occurs, what it means for democracy, and how (or if) it might be overcome.

# Notes

1. As noted in Chapter 2, Skocpol and other state theorists do not argue that states continually enjoy both autonomy and capacity. They are interested in examining the conditions under which the state has autonomy and capacity. At times state actors, operating without strong organizational resources, will bargain and negotiate with elite groups (Orloff and Skocpol 1984).

2. Nordlinger describes his three types of state autonomy in *On the Autonomy of the Democratic State* (1981). Type I Autonomy is when state and societal preferences diverge and the state chooses its preferred policy. Type II Autonomy is the case in which state and societal preferences diverge and the state tries to alter societal preferences so that they coincide. Type III Autonomy is when state and societal preferences coincide and the state pursues its preferred policy.

Krasner (1978) identifies a similar form of state capacity in which societal preferences are not taken as fixed in his discussions of political leadership.

3. It should be noted that Skocpol does touch upon the state's noncoercive powers when she notes that two members of the U.S. Department of Agriculture developed land-use plans "well before the New Deal, but neither could successfully 'sell' them to farmer's organizations or to Congress" (Skocpol and Finegold 1982, 275). However, she puts greater emphasis on the ways in which the state can "overcome" opposition rather than induce support.

4. Although Weissberg's claim that public opinion and pressure groups are thought to influence public officials (rather than the other way around) is true for most analyses of policymaking, some pluralists, like Dahl in *Who Governs,* do emphasize the role that political leadership can play in altering citizens' policy preferences. However, the point developed in this chapter and in Weissberg's analysis is that public officials often go beyond political leadership and use more direct means to try to alter citizens' preferences.

5. Weissberg details the variety of strategies that states use in trying to gain acceptance of their policies from citizens. First, he argues that the socialization process that all children are exposed to during primary education helps develop citizens who trust their elected officials and delegate authority to them. In addition, Weissberg cites evidence of the federal government's undertaking more overt strategies for gaining support for its policies. Many of these examples come from the use of propaganda and organized public relations campaigns by the military. He also cites examples like the Department of Transportation's printing a brochure in 1969 for teachers to use in their classrooms to promote Super Sonic Transport (SST) (Weissberg 1976, 228).

6. Minutes of the Hazardous Waste Planning Council, Waste Management Board, St. Paul, Minnesota, 16 September 1988.

7. Cerrell and Associates, 1984, report prepared for the California Waste Management Board.

8. Don Sandbeck, Koochiching County Commissioner, interview with author, International Falls, Minnesota, 27 September 1989.

9. Gene Ulring, County Engineer Red Lake County, interview with author, Red Lake Falls, Minnesota, 19 April 1990.

10. An additional motivation for supporting this facility was offered by Dan Joyce, a member of the Koochiching County advisory council.

If we could use this issue to take care of the metal sludges, but also use it to clean up some of the other pollution problems in our own county area. If we used that as a catalyst, that would be a real benefit, not only economically but ecologically. (Dan Joyce, member of the Koochiching County advisory council, interview with author, Littlefork, Minnesota, 28 September 1989)

11. Laurel Beager, "Group Sees Waste Site as Environmental Responsibility," *Northome Record,* 15 November 1988.

12. Jody Gross, Letter to the Editor, *International Falls Journal,* 28 April 1988,  13.

13. Bernie Hanson, Letter to the Editor, *International Falls Journal,* 3 May 1988, 7.

14. Richard N. Andrews, "Hazardous Waste Facility Siting: State Approaches," in *Dimensions of Hazardous Waste Politics and Policy,* eds. C. Davis and J. P. Lester (New York: Greenwood Press, 1988), 117–128, notes that many states have tried siting using both eminent domain and local veto.

15. Dan Reinke, "Development of a Stabilization and Containment Facility in Minnesota," paper presented at the 81st Annual Meeting of the Air Pollution Control Association, Dallas, Texas, 1988, 7.

16. Ibid., 6.

17. "Hazardous Waste Contract," *Red Lake Falls Gazette,* 10 October 1990.

18. "Hale Approves Partial Closing of the Waste Management Board Records," *Northome Record*, 9 August 1988.

19. Portney (1988) suggests that strategies to allay citizens' assessment of risk in hazardous waste siting hold some promise in gaining acceptance. Economic incentives generally do not work (Portney 1991, 1988; Elliot 1984).

20. Joseph Pavelich, Chair of Waste Management Board, 1989, "Response to *Waste Management Board Financial and Compliance Audit for the Period July 1, 1985 through October 7, 1988,*" Financial Audit Division, Office of the Legislative Auditor.

21. Letter from Terri Ann Port, Director of Facility Development, Waste Management Board, to Jody Gross, opponent of facility development in Koochiching County, 20 October 1988.

22. "Hazardous Waste Advisory Council Tours Site in Alberta," *Littlefork Times,* 14 October 1987.

23. Bruce Biggins, Koochiching County Commissioner, interview with author, International Falls, Minnesota, 26 September 1989.

24. Office of the Legislative Auditor, Financial Audit Division, 1989, *Waste Manage-*

*ment Board Financial and Compliance Audit for the Period July 1, 1985 through October 7, 1988,* 7.

25. Ibid.

26. Minutes of the Hazardous Waste Planning Council, Waste Management Board, St. Paul, Minnesota, 16 September 1988.

27. Minutes of the Waste Management Board, Crystal, Minnesota, 26 May 1988.

28. Office of the Legislative Auditor, Financial Audit Division, 1989, *Waste Management Board Financial and Compliance Audit for the Period July 1, 1985 through October 7, 1988,* 7.

29. Robert Weissberg, *Public Opinion and Popular Government* (Englewood Cliffs: Prentice-Hall, 1979), 228.

30. Memorandum, John Morely, Waste Management Board Staff, to Dennis Taylor, Administrative Manager, 4 August 1988.

31. The referendum was never held in Koochiching County because the legality of a county-run referendum was questioned. Eventually the state attorney general determined that counties could not conduct their own referenda without the approval of the state legislature.

32. In his historical account of risk management strategies, Leiss (1996) contends that too much emphasis on persuasive techniques and overt attempts to establish credibility create skepticism in the target audience. This phenomenon seems to have been at work in Minnesota's siting attempt.

33. Bobbie Wilkerling, "Northome Commissioner Talks about His Role," *International Clipper Viewpoint,* 28 December 1988.

34. "List of Counties in WMB Site Search Trimmed Down to Eight," *Red Lake Falls Gazette,* 25 November 1987.

35. Susan Boyle, resident of Koochiching County, interview with author, International Falls, Minnesota, 26 September 1989.

36. Public officials' claims that they are working in the general interest appear to be successful in other areas. Ikenberry (1988), in particular, shows how executives in the Carter administration were able to overcome the opposition of oil consumer and producer groups who opposed decontrol by arguing that decontrol would strengthen the dollar and improve the country's balance-of-trade position.

37. Letter from Terri Ann Port, Director of Facility Development, Waste Management Board, to Jody Gross, opponent of facility development in Koochiching County, 20 October 1988. In the letter Terri Port notes that not all of Dr. McQuaid-Cook's time was spent working in Koochiching County.

38. Office of the Legislative Auditor, Financial Audit Division, 1989, *Waste Management Board Financial and Compliance Audit for the Period July 1, 1985 through October 7, 1988,* 6.

39. Memorandum, Tom Johnson, Legislative Liaison to Waste Management Board staff, 23 August 1988.

40. Doris Hanson, Koochiching County Commissioner, interview with author, International Falls, Minnesota, 27 September 1989.

41. The Massachusetts siting strategy was to let private companies determine where they would site disposal facilities but to provide the opportunity for citizens to negotiate with the developers about the conditions under which they would accept a facility, including the compensation they would receive (Portney 1991; Rabe 1994).

42. "Waste Management Board in Total Control," *Littlefork Times,* 18 May 1988.

43. "Citizens at Northome Waste Meeting Express Opposition to Hazardous Waste Site," *Littlefork Times,* 3 August 1988.

44. Rita and Steve Linder, Letter to the Editor, *Oklee Herald,* 18 May 1988.

By starting with discussions of burden sharing and developing a more integrated approach to waste management, the WMB might have been able to reduce the feeling that urban counties were dumping their problem on rural counties. I discuss this further in Chapter 5. See Rabe (1994) also for a discussion of burden sharing in Alberta and its absence in Minnesota.

45. Don Sandbeck, County Commissioner, Koochiching County, interview with author, International Falls, Minnesota, 27 September 1989.

46. Bruce Biggins, County Commissioner, Koochiching County, interview with author, International Falls, Minnesota, 26 September 1989.

47. For an in-depth look at the relationship between public opinion and policy at the state level, see Erikson, Wright, and McIver (1993).

# CHAPTER 4

# State Officials and Citizens: The Siting Deadlock

The role of citizens in policymaking has long been a source of debate within American politics. As far back as the founding of the country, the Federalists and the Anti-Federalists deliberated about the influence that citizens should have over the conduct of politics. In accordance with our Federalist tradition, some contemporary political observers have urged caution in allowing widespread participation on the part of citizens in policymaking.[1] Such critics argue that citizens are not able to grasp complex political or technical problems, think in sophisticated ways about policy decisions, or look beyond their narrow self-interest in making policy choices.[2]

This skeptical view of citizens' capacity to participate in politics is challenged by those who hold a more sanguine view of citizens and their abilities to reason and make political judgments. In their writings, Robert Dahl (1989) and Charles Lindblom (1990) advance the argument that citizens are able to make political choices that are at least as, if not more, reasonable and defensible as those of policy experts. Other democratic theorists like Fishkin (1995) and Barber (1984) argue for the importance of deliberation to meaningful democratic decision-making and urge the design of political institutions that can facilitate citizen participation in this deliberation.

Those who are skeptical of citizens' ability to effectively participate in politics maintain an optimistic view of policy experts' moral and instrumental knowledge (e.g., Beckman 1973; Ophuls 1977, 1992). Policy experts who remain objective and committed to scientific understandings of policy issues can stand above partisan politics and make informed judgments about how public policy should be conducted. On the issue of risk management and regulation (as in the potential harm caused by asbestos), Breyer (1993) and Margolis (1996) give spirited defenses of a technocratic solution to regulation by arguing that experts are demonstrably better at understanding risks than are citizens. Margolis's general claim is that citizens' patterned response to environmental regulation is to "Do No Harm," that is, they want to avoid all risks and are not really attentive to the additional costs that arise from this mindset. Experts, according to Margolis, approach risk management from a perspective of "Waste Not, Want Not" and are much better at thinking about trade-offs between the costs and benefits associated with the reduction or elimination of certain risks. Breyer holds a similar view of experts and citizens and proposes a board of experts to determine costs and benefits associated with regulation of risks, thus providing a check on what he sees as excessive spending by lawmakers who try to eliminate chemicals or other risks that have a very low probability of causing harm.

At the same time these skeptics view citizens as overly emotional and self-serving, and therefore unable to participate in politics in a way that will allow society to achieve its "best interest." The pathologies of political participation are thought to be especially troublesome on issues like hazardous waste policy, whereby citizens' lack of expertise, coupled with the Nimby syndrome, lead to obstructionism and parochialism on the part of citizens. Only through expert decision-making can these problems associated with citizen participation be avoided and the collective good be attained.

It is through the development of state autonomy and capacity that state actors can resist the pressures of external political actors and pursue policies which they believe will best serve the interest of the public writ large. For example, Heclo argues that social problem-solving is aided by state officials' willingness to "puzzle . . . on society's behalf" (1974, 305). Krasner makes this argument regarding the beneficent nature of state decision-making even more explicitly in claiming that public officials act in the "interest of" the community (1978, 12).

Robert Dahl and Charles Lindblom contest this view of expert decision-making as serving the general welfare, as well as the claim that citizens are unsophisticated and myopic in making policy choices.[3] They argue that policy experts are not neutral with respect to their policy choices since they are predisposed to certain outcomes and choices by virtue of the training that they receive and the environment in which they work. For example, experts tend to be confident that the technology that they are dealing with will work as designed and not be subject to unanticipated mechanical or design problems. In addition, in making policy choices, policy experts often fail to recognize the implicit value choices that are embedded in "technical decision-making." According to Dahl, "[o]rdinarily, policy judgments require an assessment of *both* uncertainties *and* trade-offs. In these instances, the superior competence of experts diminishes to the vanishing point" (1989, 75). For example, nuclear weapons experts focus policy discussions on mutually assured destruction as a technical solution to arms build-ups, without simultaneously discussing the ethical issues implicit in such a strategy or the social and economic costs to building the weaponry to achieve Mutually Assured Destruction (MAD) (Dahl 1989, 75). Similarly, Lindblom (1990) expresses doubt that the narrow training of policy experts will help them cope with the complexity and interrelatedness of problems they face in making policy decisions.

At the same time, Dahl, Lindblom, and other advocates of citizen participation challenge the assumption that citizens are uninformed and obstructionist when participating in politics. For example, Fishkin (1995) argues that citizens have the capacity to reason effectively about policy issues but simply lack the institutional mechanisms for doing so, and when put in a setting like his deliberative poll, they are able to engage and meaningfully consider important policy issues. Kraft and Clary (1991) directly examine this issue of citizen rationality in policymaking on issues of radioactive waste disposal and find that citizens are not myopic and irrational in making policy decisions. They examined the content of public testimony on a proposed low-level radioactive waste disposal site and discovered that citizens participating in the debates were familiar with the ideas and language used by policy experts, offered concrete and plausible alternatives to the Department of Energy's proposals, and thought about the potential impact of the facility on society in general—not just its impact on their own communities. Also, Cronin (1989) presents evidence from public opinion surveys which shows that those voting in a referendum generally understand the issues and become increasingly informed as the day to vote gets closer. In their in-depth analysis of public opinion over time, Page and Shapiro (1992) find that collectively citizens are able to form reasonable perceptions and preferences for important policy issues. Evidence such as this supports Dahl and Lindblom's belief in citizens' ability to make informed judgments about policy issues.

Hazardous waste siting is an important issue on which to examine these debates regarding the utility of technocratic and democratic decision-making. On issues like hazardous waste, where decision-making involves technology and materials that pose some risk to citizens, it is likely that citizens' and experts' views of good policy will diverge. Recent evidence suggests that this gap emerges out of differences in how each (decision-makers and citizens) assess risks from potential environmental hazards.[4] One analyst of these differences suggested that citizens react more to highly visible events like hazardous waste siting than to less conspicuous threats such as auto emissions.[5] A survey revealed that citizens rank hazardous waste sites as one of the greatest risks to public safety, whereas EPA officials placed them in the middle of their rankings of environmental hazards.[6] As a result of these differences,

> the public is eager to discuss siting, but does not believe what the so-called "experts" tell them. Scientists, engineers, government officials and industrial representatives have little credibility when it comes to siting hazardous waste facilities. (Greenberg 1984, 165)

Thus the hazardous waste issue allows us to examine how state officials pursue their policy objectives while being challenged by citizens. We can then observe whether policy experts develop policies which are rationally constructed and in the general interest, or whether citizens themselves can offer insightful and useful alternatives to the policies being advanced by state officials (rather than being emotional and irrational, as they are often portrayed).

This examination of Minnesota's hazardous waste policy will attempt to provide a more detailed understanding of the evaluations of hazardous waste policy by citizens and experts, and the problems that arise for democratic decision-making when they are in conflict. Is the political stalemate that characterizes hazardous waste siting evidence of democracy run amok, where citizens and other political actors can veto policies that are in their best interest? Or is the stalemate evidence that democracy works, as citizens challenge and contest the claims of policy experts and uncover flaws or inequities in their policy prescriptions?

Minnesota provides a good case for comparing the competing views of citizen and expert rationality. Minnesota has a state government with a reputation for effective problem-solving, and we would therefore expect its policy prescriptions to be comprehensive and persuasive. On the hazardous waste issue the state's initiatives were being challenged primarily by rural counties, and this is where we would least expect citizens in the community to have the technical expertise to develop a convincing critique of the state's proposals.

This chapter will examine the debate between citizens in two rural counties and Minnesota's Waste Management Board and clarify the lessons we can draw from this case regarding the utility of democratic and technocratic decision-making. I use survey data, interviews, and newspaper accounts to show the commonalities and differences between citizens and policymakers. First, I describe the differences in perceptions between citizens and state officials about key issues (including risks and benefits) associated with the facility. Next, using survey data, I test whether the perceptions of the facility found in interviews and newspapers are equally influential in citizens' thinking, or if some weigh more heavily.[7] By providing detailed evidence of the debate between citizens and policy experts, we can assess the claims of skeptics and defenders of citizen participation. Do policy experts reveal a deeper and more sophisticated understanding of the instrumental issues, or are citizens' judgments on par with those of experts? Does the debate hinge on normative issues and do experts reveal a better understanding of these normative issues, or are citizens' views equally compelling?

## The Sources of Disagreement: Citizens and State Officials

In 1990 I conducted open-ended interviews with activist and nonactivist citizens in the community and a random sample mail survey in each county, yielding 370 respondents in Koochiching County and 337 in Red Lake County.[8] I use the qualitative findings from the interviews and the results from the surveys of county residents to provide a composite of citizen opinion about the facility, its associated risks and benefits, and where it should be located. I also describe citizens' trust of state officials and their attitudes toward future policy alternatives.[9] In this section I compare this summary evaluation of citizen opinion to interviews with key policymakers about the need for and safety of the facility.

Although the main purpose of this section is to compare the opinions of state officials to those of citizens, I will note important differences or similarities between the two counties when they relate to Nimby issues. As a starting point, it is important to note that despite the interest in the facility among county officials in both Koochiching County and Red Lake County, opposition to the facility among county residents was quite strong and highly visible. In Red Lake County (which was five months from a binding referendum on the issue at the time of the survey) the survey showed 26.7 percent wanted the facility, whereas 64.9 percent were opposed to it. (See Table 4.1.) In Koochiching County, which was no longer a candidate for the facility at the time of the survey, 18.6 percent said that they had favored the facility and 78.6 percent had been opposed to it. Although there is a significant difference in the mean response in each county, it is clear that opposition in both counties was strong. With this general evaluation in mind, I will focus in more detail on the sources of disagreement between citizens and policymakers: perceptions of risk, trust, location of the facility, and policy options.

Perceptions of Risk

There is strong evidence from studies of other siting attempts around the country that the assessment of risk has an important influence on how people evaluate a facility.[10] This general claim seems to have been true in Minnesota as well. The key risks from the facility for citizens in Red Lake and Koochiching Counties were groundwater contamination and transportation of the hazardous waste.

Citizens in both counties believed that the facility posed some threat to the groundwater and that contamination of it would be devastating to the communities. As Velma Oakland, an elementary school teacher in Red Lake County and one of the founders of Concerned Citizens Against Hazardous Waste, explained:

I chose to live up here for the clean water and the clean air, and I guess that is what we have going for us in northern Minnesota. We've got the environment, the health, all these different things going for us. If they bring a site like this in, what could happen as far as groundwater contamination?[11]

This belief that the facility would threaten the groundwater was widely held. In the survey citizens were asked whether they believed "the chances

Table 4.1 Responses to the Citizen Surveys in Koochiching and Red Lake Counties

| Question / Percent Who | Koochiching | | | Red Lake | | |
|---|---|---|---|---|---|---|
| | Agree/ Favor | Disagree/ Oppose | DK | Agree/ Favor | Disagree/ Oppose | DK |
| 1. Did you favor or oppose the building of the facility? | 18.6% | 78.6% | 2.8% | 26.7% | 64.9% | 8.3%* |
| 2. The chances of the hazardous waste facility polluting the ground water were high. | 69.0 | 21.2 | 9.8 | 66.7 | 25.1 | 8.2 |
| 3. The chance of hazardous waste accidentally spilling during transport to the treatment facility would have been small. | 27.0 | 61.9 | 11.1 | 37.6 | 54.2 | 8.3* |
| 4. On technical issues like the disposal of hazardous waste, I trust the state to look out for my best interest and the interest of Minnesota. | 41.5 | 46.0 | 12.0 | 39.6 | 50.0 | 10.8 |
| 5. The state should build a facility closer to the Twin Cities because that is where most of the hazardous waste is produced. | 77.0 | 12.1 | 11.0 | 72.2 | 16.2 | 11.7 |
| 6. The facility is necessary for the State of Minnesota to meet its long-term goals of a clean environment. | 52.4 | 31.4 | 16.3 | 34.9 | 49.6 | 15.5* |
| 7. The state should continue looking for a county to take the facility because Minnesota needs this facility. | 51.6 | 31.4 | 16.4 | 40.0 | 45.0 | 15.0* |
| 8. The state should prohibit the manufacturing of products which create hazardous waste. | 41.1 | 41.8 | 17.1 | 53.5 | 35.4 | 11.2* |
| 9. The state should continue shipping waste to other states because they have the facilities to safely dispose of these wastes. | 46.8 | 32.9 | 20.3 | 46.3 | 32.8 | 20.9 |

Source: Author's survey.
*=Indicates a significant difference between the two counties' responses based on ANOVA (Analysis of Variance) ($p < .05$).
DK=Don't Know.

of the hazardous waste facility polluting the groundwater were high." In both counties nearly 70 percent of those surveyed agreed with this statement.

The concerns of citizens in the candidate counties about transportation coincided with their attitudes regarding water contamination. If the facility had been built in either county, most of the untreated waste would have been trucked approximately 250 miles for treatment and storage. The traffic was estimated at four or five truckloads per day (Dames and Moore 1990). Citizens were concerned that these trucks would be traveling through their communities over two-lane highways in weather that can be quite severe in the winter.[12] As one of the survey respondents reported, "knowing the accident rates of commercial trucking and the quality of the roads to be traveled and the condition of the roads in the winter, I would have expected to see a spill of the untreated waste in a lake, river, or water-filled ditch along the way."[13]

The survey revealed that this concern about the safety of transporting the waste was widespread in the counties. In response to the statement that "the chances of hazardous waste spilling during transport to the treatment facility would have been small," 54.2 percent disagreed and 37.6 percent agreed in Red Lake County. In Koochiching 61.9 percent disagreed and 27 percent agreed with the statement. As Table 4. 1 shows, there is a significant difference in the responses from the two counties, but ironically, in Red Lake County, which was still a candidate for the facility at the time of the survey, residents were less concerned about spills than those of Koochiching County.

Citizens' assessments of risk differed starkly from the risk assessment of decision-makers at the WMB. Not unexpectedly, state actors were quite confident that the facility posed very little threat to the groundwater and that the risks of an accident threatening the population were minimal. Representatives from the Waste Management Board used adjectives like "over designed" and "overkill" in terms of the environmental safety design of the facility.[14] In the minds of policymakers, the citizens' fears about groundwater contamination and an accident during transport were unfounded. Furthermore, the WMB and supporters within the county tried to minimize the perceived threat of an accident by arguing that the transportation of the waste constituted less of a threat than the transportation of other chemicals. In particular, they argued that relative to the transportation of gasoline, that of hazardous waste was a minimal risk. The waste that would have been trucked to the facility was not flammable and had no toxic fumes, unlike gasoline. And if a spill did occur, the waste could easily be put back into a tanker truck and transported to the facility for treatment. As Gene Ulring, the Red Lake County Engineer and one of the strong proponents of the facility, argued:

> Local farmers are a much, much greater threat, with pesticide spills or gasoline spills. This waste is not that volatile, and the fumes won't kill you. Some of this stuff hauled up and down the freeway every day will.[15]

Citizens and community leaders in neighboring counties which would have been on the transportation route were equally concerned about the risk of an accident while the waste was en route. In Beltrami County, just south of Koochiching County, the county board passed a resolution asking the Koochiching board to allow it some input into the decision-making. They argued that they had a legitimate right to have access to the decision-making process since the waste would be transported across most of Beltrami while only the southern tip of Koochiching (around the Northome area) would have any waste passing through it.

Despite evidence of some disagreement within the county regarding the risks associated with the facility, the majority of citizens perceived the facility as a threat to their environment. These perceptions are at odds with the more sanguine attitudes of state officials about the possible risk. These differences in perceptions between state officials and citizens in Minnesota are consistent with other research comparing citizens and public officials across the states (Greenberg 1984), as well as with comparisons between U.S. citizens and national decision-makers. Recent analyses suggest that the differences in the decision-makers' and citizens' assessment of risks from potential environmental hazards are rooted in different epistemological frameworks—that is, different understandings of what knowledge is most relevant or important.

Cvetkovich and Earle (1992) argue that experts view environmental hazards from an *objectivist* perspective. Objectivists emphasize the physical characteristics of facilities and probabilistic assessments of risk. They also assume "that for any given hazard there is one true risk, usually defined on the basis of the probability and the severity of negative outcomes, and that it can be assessed" (Cvetkovich and Earle 1992, 5). Citizens, on the other hand, are more likely to approach hazardous waste from a *constructivist* perspective. Citizens who rely on this perspective to evaluate risk will think more contextually about the risk from a hazardous waste facility and rely on information that is not merely probabilistic. "Risk perceptions are socially constructed in the sense that individuals make inferences and reach conclusions by giving meaning to uncertain and ambiguous information on the basis of communication with others" (Cvetkovich and Earle 1992, 6). Thus citizens are likely to take seriously psychological or emotional concerns about the facility as well as concerns about the social impact of a hazardous waste disposal facility on a community. As an example of the consequences of the difference between these two types of thinking, citizens are more likely than experts to see a hazardous waste facility as incompatible with a local economy that emphasizes tourism or agriculture.

The identification of these differences in risk assessment raises an important challenge for those who wish to exclude citizens from deliberations on hazardous waste siting. It is difficult to claim that the objectivist perspective endorsed by policy experts is superior to or more legitimate than the constructivist perspective adopted by citizens. Likewise, it is unlikely that citizens or experts will easily change their disparate approaches to risk assessment. If meaningful deliberation on hazardous waste policy is going to take place, both kinds of information must be taken seriously (Cvetkovich and Earle 1992; Freudenburg and Pastor 1992; Kunreuther and Slovic 1996; Leiss 1996).[16]

These differences are also consistent with other research on risk perception in which experts and citizens are thought to operate with different approaches regarding risk assessment. Experts tend to rely on probabilistic risk assessment, in which they calculate the likelihood that an accident will happen, such as waste from a hazardous waste treatment facility getting into the groundwater. Citizens, on the other hand, tend to assess risk by asking what will happen if an accident should occur (Slovic et al. 1982). Although these issues were not addressed specifically in my survey, this claim that citizens and experts begin to assess risk by asking different questions is consistent with the survey results, which showed that citizens were very concerned about the risk to themselves and their community whereas experts felt that these risks were minimal.

Who Benefits?

An issue related to risk assessment is the evaluation of who will benefit and who will potentially be hurt by this facility. State officials clearly believed that the counties would benefit from the compensation package that they were offering, as did a majority of county commissioners. In addition, they perceived that the facility would contribute to the general welfare of Minnesota through the safe disposal of some of the hazardous waste produced in the state. Finally, they assumed that Minnesota industry would benefit from a safe disposal facility that would be relatively close to Minnesota producers, thus reducing shipping costs for some and providing a measure of insurance against future liability for others.[17]

State officials in Minnesota were not naïve and blindly optimistic about the facility. Some did recognize that residents adjacent to the facility had potentially the most to lose. Also, the benefits package provided resources to the county at large rather than explicit benefits to those in close proximity to the facility. But state officials tried to push for some compensation for those directly adjacent to the facility site:

> I think clearly the people who stand to lose would be the immediate neighbors of the facility. Simply because the way the benefits tend to work out, they tend to be benefits that are directed more to the community at large, while people who are living immediately adjacent to it, they're the ones that will be most worried about it, have to live with it on a day-to-day basis. And they may not perceive themselves as sharing the benefits. They may see themselves as having all of the risk but few of the benefits, which I think is a valid argument.[18]

Even though state officials were sensitive to the fact that some people were at greater risk from the facility, overall the perceptions of who would benefit and who would be hurt varied between state officials and citizens. For example, whereas state officials thought that this facility would benefit future generations of Minnesotans, a majority of citizens in Red Lake County thought that this facility might harm future generations. In addition, most county residents did not think that the state as a whole would benefit from the construction of the stabilization and containment facility.[19]

Trust

On some public policy issues citizens are willing to put their trust in public officials and delegate decision-making to them. For example, few people challenge the procedures for licensing doctors and nurses. However, this kind of trust is notably absent from decisions about hazardous waste, particularly on its siting aspects.[20] In a paper written to describe the strategies used by the state in trying to site Minnesota's facility, Daniel Reinke of Minnesota's Waste Management Board emphasized the importance of gaining trust to successfully siting a hazardous waste facility (Reinke 1988).

However, trust is difficult to build on hazardous waste issues because the potential damage is quite severe and an accident would have an immediate impact on neighboring communities. Recent reports about public officials' failure to adequately warn citizens about the risks of potentially dangerous facilities only serve to heighten this suspicion (as in the case of the radiation leaks from the Hanover, Washington, nuclear facility).

In its attempts to site a facility in northern Minnesota, state officials not only had to contend with fears generated from mismanagement at the national level, but also had to work to overcome suspicion toward WMB personnel from an earlier siting attempt. In 1983 the WMB investigated crystalline bedrock disposal as an alternative to the more conventional landfill disposal. This method required locating crystalline bedrock deposits in the state, boring holes into the bedrock, and injecting hazardous waste into the cavities for long-term storage.

Exploratory drilling to examine the feasibility of this method met with vehement opposition from some citizens in northern Minnesota. One of the exploration sites was in the Ash Lake area, located on the border of Koochiching and St. Louis Counties. State officials were hoping to take drilling equipment onto the site to make some test borings and check the stability of the granite. However, citizens opposed to this facility challenged the drilling team and the federal marshals who had come to escort them by blocking their path to the site. Eventually the drilling team and the marshals withdrew from the site.[21]

Although the Ash Lake tests were not a central part of the debate about the stabilization and containment facility, contention about them did arise in some of the early discussions about the new facility. People remembered the Ash Lake incident two years later when the WMB was in the area trying to assure residents of the safety of this new stabilization and containment facility. In particular, Bruce Biggins, the Koochiching County commissioner opposed to the facility, used Ash Lake as a rallying point for opposition to the facility by drawing parallels between the two attempts.

It was an involuntary siting process in which they were telling us that the safest technology was to drill holes down to the crystalline bedrock and dump hazardous materials down those holes. Common sense tells you that's not a good idea. We're dealing with the same set of players in this issue, so it's hard to trust them just because this is a new game.[22]

Because of lingering resentment over the Ash Lake tests the state faced a formidable challenge in trying to win the trust of local citizens from the outset of the process.

The evidence from the survey suggests that the state never successfully overcame citizens' initial suspicions. In both counties most respondents disagreed with this statement: "On technical issues like the disposal of hazardous waste, I trust the state government to look out for my best interest and the interest of Minnesota." In Koochiching the distribution was 46 percent disagreement to 41 percent agreement. In Red Lake the percentages were 50 percent disagreeing and 39.2 percent agreeing.

Not unexpectedly, people who supported the facility seemed more willing to accept the state's claims about the safety of it. Ron Linder of the Concerned Citizens for a Clean Environment claimed, "We're living in a high-tech society. We've got to have faith in these people [the Waste Management Board and the developer, Ecostar] whether we want to or not, because the average person just doesn't understand these things" (Beager 1988). Dan Joyce, one of the members of the Koochiching advisory council, echoed these sentiments. He argued that the amount of information that had to be digested to make an informed decision was overwhelming. He felt that the state could be trusted to build the facility safely and that the benefits the state was offering made the facility attractive to him.

In Minnesota's siting effort lack of trust in the state appeared to weigh heavily in people's evaluation of the stabilization and containment facility. This is consistent with other studies of siting decisions and trust. In their study of citizen attitudes about a proposed hazardous waste incinerator in West Virginia, Hunter and Leyden (1995) argue that trust is a key factor in citizens' support of a hazardous waste facility and that mistrust does not necessarily indicate that citizens are afflicted by the Nimby syndrome. In fact, citizens' mistrust of government officials is rather widespread these days, making it difficult to contend that citizens who are suspicions of state decision-makers on hazardous waste issues are unusual or exceptionally troublesome.[23] Lindblom (1990, 1993) in particular suggests that skepticism and a willingness to challenge public officials is critical to effective problem-solving. A greater danger lies in like-minded thinking and an easy consensus.

## Location of the Facility

Discussions with local opponents of the facility and written comments from the surveys revealed that another principal concern of citizens was the location of the facility. Many people felt that the facility should be located closer to the Twin Cities. Citizens opposed to the facility appealed to decision-makers' sense of fairness and argued that since most of the waste was produced in the Twin Cities, metro area residents should assume the risk.[24] From the opponents' perspective, the jobs and income that are generated from industrial production are the benefits that come with hazardous waste and those who receive such benefits should bear the majority of the risk.

This belief that the facility belonged closer to the Twin Cities was reiterated in the responses to survey questions as well. Koochiching residents were asked a set of questions about alternatives for coping with the hazardous waste problem once the county board had withdrawn its candidacy. Seventy-seven percent of the respondents agreed or strongly agreed that the facility should be built closer to the Twin Cities. In Red Lake County residents were asked to respond to policy alternatives if the facility were voted down in the referendum. Seventy-two percent of respondents agreed or strongly agreed that the facility should be located nearer the metropolitan area.

The fact that there is not a significant difference between the two counties is an important finding, one which challenges the classic Nimby claims. Respondents in Koochiching County, who knew at the time of the survey that the facility was unlikely to be located in their county, agreed with Red Lake County residents that it should be near the Twin Cities. Thus Red Lake County residents' desire to site the facility near the Twin Cities cannot simply be dismissed as a desire to have it anywhere but near them.

Most state officials, on the other hand, felt that Minnesota had a moral obligation to ensure long-term protection of the environment, and this obligation justified siting the facility anywhere in the state. All Minnesotans, they argued, had to assume the responsibility of disposing of hazardous waste and work toward a solution that would safely contain it. Similarly, supporters of the facility in the counties argued that this was an issue in which all citizens must work together to protect the environment, and that the facility was the best way of doing this.

I think it is time we all take responsibility for the "garbage" [heavy metals] we produce. It doesn't make a whole lot of difference if Twin

Cities waste is brought to Koochiching if every effort is made to protect the environment and citizens. I am a realist—I know that we have space and the Twin Cities doesn't.[25]

Both state officials and supporters of the facility insisted that citizens in remote areas were beneficiaries of industrial production of things like computer chips and therefore were contributors to the hazardous waste problem.

The guy living on 600 acres up here is as responsible for that waste as the guy living on the 13th floor of a Minneapolis high-rise. Just more individuals down there. And a lot of them are relatives of mine and a lot of them are relatives of everybody else who lives here.[26]

The WMB and its supporters' position was that the facility was necessary to protect the environment from degradation due to improper storage of hazardous waste. They believed that Minnesota should not continue to shirk its responsibility to pass on a viable ecosystem to future generations and therefore must use prudent and available technologies to contain toxics which might otherwise damage the environment.

This sense that the facility would protect future generations of Minnesotans was not evident in the survey responses of citizens of Red Lake County, who did not believe that facility "would benefit future generations." (Fifty-two and a half percent thought that future generations would be hurt by the facility.) In addition, most county residents did not see the state as a whole benefitting from the construction of the stabilization and containment facility. (Only 15.7 percent thought that the state as a whole would benefit from the facility.)[27]

On the issue of the location of the facility, citizens challenged both the state's normative and instrumental claims about the appropriateness of a hazardous waste facility in rural Minnesota. Although the citizens' desire to have the facility located closer to the Twin Cities could be viewed as simply a manifestation of the Nimby syndrome, the issue of fairness does confound the claim. It is difficult for state officials to insist that they have better insight into the value trade-off between siting the facility near the metro area versus in a rural area, since this choice requires a determination of who should appropriately bear the risk. The instrumental challenge that citizens offered to the location—namely that it was safer to build the facility near the source of production to reduce transportation risks and shipping costs—carried added weight, since these ideas were supported by the business community as well.[28] Although these location issues seem on the surface to be a classic example of the Nimby syndrome, the pathologies and narrow-minded thinking that critics attribute to the Nimby syndrome become less clear as details of cases like this one are examined.

Policy Options

Part of the disagreement between citizens and state decision-makers over hazardous waste policy stemmed from the state's commitment to the facility. State decision-makers repeatedly argued that no matter how much recycling, reclamation, and reduction was done, there would always be a core residue of waste that must be safely managed. Therefore, according to state officials, Minnesota should provide a means by which this waste could be safely treated and stored.

However, there did not appear to be a strong consensus among citizens for continuing to look for a facility once this siting effort was over. In Koochiching County a majority of survey respondents felt that the facility was "necessary for the state of Minnesota to meet its long-term goal of a clean environment." (See Table 4.1. Survey results were 52 percent to 31 percent.) However, in Red Lake County there was a significant difference in support for the facility. Respondents there, on average, were unconvinced of the need for the facility, with 50 percent opposing and 35 percent supporting. Similarly, in another question, respondents were asked whether officials should continue looking for a site somewhere in the state if the facility was not built in their county. Again, Koochiching citizens were generally in support of continuing the search, whereas Red Lake citizens were not. Thus there did not seem to be an overriding consensus among citizens that the state should continue looking for a site, and as the discussion of location issues earlier indicated, if the state was going to pursue siting the facility, citizens and business groups thought that it should be located near the source of production.

In the debates over the need for the facility some county residents proposed a ban on products that leave hazardous waste as a by-product. Sue Boyle, a Koochiching County resident and member of the advisory council, argued in support of a ban, saying that she would happily give up the chrome bumper on her next car as a way of reducing the amount of hazardous waste in the state.[29] (Residuals from chrome-plating are one of the primary wastes that Minnesota industry produces.) However, Jean Moser from the Red Lake advisory council claimed that she was not interested in giving up chrome faucets and bathroom fixtures as a way of reducing the waste stream, and that treating the waste and safely disposing of it was preferable to a ban on certain products.[30]

This issue of banning products to reduce hazardous waste in the state was addressed in the survey as well. Respondents were asked if they thought the state should ban products which led to the production of hazardous waste. In Red Lake County 54 percent versus 35 percent of respondents were willing to accept a ban of products. In contrast to this clear preference in Red Lake, the citizens in Koochiching County were evenly divided over this issue. (State officials generally did not consider the ban a viable alternative, partly because they felt that citizens would be unwilling to part with products that would be banned, but also because they felt that it would jeopardize Minnesota's business climate.)

Citizens opposed to the facility also argued that not enough work had been done by the state to promote waste recycling, reclamation, and reductions in the amount of waste produced. Jody Gross, one of the organizers of the Northland Concerned Citizens in Koochiching County, suggested that a reduction in the waste stream seemed a logical first step to addressing Minnesota's hazardous waste problem. Once waste reduction was given a chance to work, the Waste Management Board would have a better idea of the future demand for waste disposal within the state.[31] The Minnesota Technical Assistance Program (MnTap) was the state's principal waste reduction program at this time. It began in 1984 to provide technical and financial assistance primarily to small businesses to help them reduce their waste generation. (The state's waste reduction efforts are discussed in more detail in Chapter 5.)

Finally, residents in the two counties did not share the same moral commitments as state officials with regard to shipping waste out of state. State decision-makers were reluctant to continue the current practice of shipping the waste out of state, in part because they felt Minnesota had a moral obligation to manage its own waste.

I've noticed in my time that there's almost a moral dimension to this. We've sometimes found ourselves making the argument that we're making these inorganic residual wastes and taking them to other states. But we should be taking care of that ourselves: "we should be responsible for our own wastes" sort of argument.[32]

Respondents were not similarly persuaded, and generally agreed that shipping the waste to out-of-state landfills was an acceptable alternative to building a facility in the state. (Data in both counties showed 46 percent approving to 33 percent disapproving, with no significant difference.) Citizens who opposed the facility argued that Minnesota's economy was based more on agriculture and services than on manufacturing, and they did not want to see the state become a leader in hazardous waste disposal. Although this policy preference could be viewed as evidence of Nimby thinking, it can also be seen as consistent with citizens' general skepticism that the state needed this facility. In addition, there was no relationship between respondents' opposition/support for the facility in their county and their support for shipping the waste out of state. This also indicates that citizens did not have a simple Nimby response to the facility.

As this contrast between county residents and state officials reveals, the differences in opinion between the two are rooted as much in normative issues as in technical ones. For example, citizens were concerned about the issues of risk and who should bear it, and the trade-off between recycling and disposal of hazardous waste, whereas state officials were more concerned with the state's taking responsibility for the hazardous waste it produced and discarding it in a disposal facility.

State officials often did not recognize the normative underpinnings of these differences but saw the conflict as attributable to the lack of citizen rationality. Thus they viewed citizen participation in decision-making with skepticism:

> And then the public tends to make sort of a visceral decision, about this is bad or this is good, sort of gut reasons. And then they use the information process as a way of gathering evidence to make their case. I just see this time and time again. You'll have people say that I've spent hours and hours and hours reading this material and studying this. You can kind of tell that the reason that they have spent hours and hours on it is because they didn't like it and so they read the material with a prejudiced eye, prejudiced against it. And similarly, we've had people who've seen the economic benefits in this for their county, and they pick up the material and they read it with a prejudiced eye toward accepting it.[33]

This skepticism of citizen participation is not limited to state officials in Minnesota. In a survey of state hazardous waste administrators around the country Davis (1984–1985) finds that overall respondents showed considerable reluctance to incorporate citizen participation in hazardous waste siting. Public officials tend to believe that solutions to technical problems can be engineered, but this optimism is not shared by citizens. As a result, public officials often discount the instrumental objections of citizens, and they tend not to see or take seriously the normative challenges that citizens put forth.

State officials and many academic observers consistently see citizen opposition as emanating from parochial, uninformed, and overly emotional thinking. Despite the pervasiveness of the Nimby syndrome in academic writing and public debates over siting decisions, it should in fact be viewed with caution. The danger of invoking Nimby arguments too quickly is that legitimate objections may get dismissed as parochialism and give state officials the moral high ground in debates. Opponents to facilities are accused of narrow self-interest, whereas public officials are depicted as far-sighted individuals trying to overcome the pettiness of citizens.

In scrutinizing the state's claims about the need for and viability of the facility, citizens developed some important challenges, ones that the state could not easily rebut. For example, the state's own calculations of profitability revealed that the facility was only marginally economically feasible because stabilization and containment is a costlier method than landfill disposal. It was not clear that the state could run this facility at capacity without Minnesota Mining and Manufacturing (3M) participating, since the waste from 3M's incinerator constituted more than 25 percent of the inorganic waste produced in the state. However, as noted in Chapter 2, 3M's participation was not guaranteed, since it was shipping its waste to Illinois at a significantly lower price per ton than the fees projected for the Minnesota facility and it was likely to find other out-of-state disposal options should the Illinois facility shut down. Because of the higher cost associated with stabilization and containment, the state would have to subsidize the cost of disposal for 3M and other waste producers in the first years of operation of the facility to make it economically viable for them to use it (Minnesota Waste Management Board 1988). Finally, calculations of profitability would only hold up if the level of waste remained relatively constant over the subsequent twenty years and future recycling and reclamation programs did not significantly reduce the amount of waste produced. If the waste stream were reduced, the facility would be viable only if the price of disposal rose significantly across the country. Through their opposition and ultimately their veto of the facility, citizens prevented the state from investing in a facility that was of questionable need, a potential drain on state resources, and a disincentive to recycling, reclamation, and reduction.

## Data Analysis

This examination of public opinion with regard to the proposed hazardous waste site in Minnesota establishes a variety of factors which come into play in citizens' evaluations. Many of these factors, such as the perception of risk from the facility, give some indication of why citizens and state officials might be at odds over this issue. Thus far these factors have been treated as independent influences on the citizens' evaluation of the facility. This section will attempt to examine these factors jointly to better understand how they work together or in opposition in explaining citizens' opinions on the state's policy.

The overview of citizen opinion in the previous section revealed that among the most important issues for citizens were the risk that the facility posed, the economic benefits, the location of the facility, and the amount of trust that citizens had in state officials. To examine the interrelationship among these factors I rely on structural equation analysis. The benefit of structural equations is that they allow for the modeling of complex relationships among the factors thought to influence citizens' thinking on this issue. Unlike single equation models, in which all the factors are assumed to have a direct influence on the dependent variable, structural equations allow us to examine feedback, indirect effects, and simultaneous effects.

Since several of the factors thought to influence citizens' opinions are not directly measured by a single survey question, the analysis includes a measurement model as well as the structural equations. The techniques for this type of measurement and structural equation analysis, also known as covariance models, are now well developed (Jöreskog and Sörbom 1989; Bentler 1980). Briefly, the central assumption behind measurement theory as it relates to survey questions is that respondents' underlying attitudes can be measured through several survey questions which tap the different dimensions of their attitude. For example, people's response to a survey question about trust in government is strongly influenced by their more general thinking about trust, but this is not observable from one simple survey question. The relationship between the survey response and the latent concept of TRUST is then specified, using the latent concept as an independent variable that explains the dependent variables, their survey responses to the trust questions.

In the measurement model (Figure 4.1) three of the latent factors are measured through multiple survey responses. (For a list of the questions associated with the variable names, see Appendix B.) First, the citizens' perceptions of the risk that the facility poses for them (RISK) are thought to be related to the survey questions about the threat the facility poses for the local water supply (WATER), the chances of a spill during transportation (TRANSP), the impact that the facility might have on tourism in Koochiching (and on the farm economy in Red Lake) (TOUR), and the possible erosion of property values (PROP).

It is important to note that the survey question asking people about their views on the money (MONEY) that the county would receive was highly related to their perceptions about risks (RISK). The robustness of this relationship was tested in a variety of models and it was consistent. This indicates that citizens viewed the compensation through their perceptions about risk and, on the whole, felt that the compensation was an inappropriate exchange for accepting the facility. (The negative relationship between opinions about compensation and opinions regarding the facility is evidence that citizens felt that the exchange was inappropriate. Those who opposed the facility did not approve of the compensation package.)[34] Because the

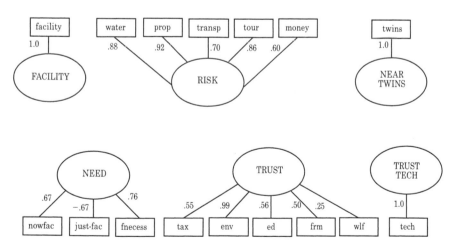

*Figure 4.1* Measurement Model for Koochiching County

variables are so highly related to the MONEY variable, it is specified in the measurement model as an indicator of perceptions about risk.

Several survey responses were also thought to measure citizens' evaluation of the need for the facility (NEED). Respondents' overall evaluations of the need for the facility were measured by questions about whether there was enough hazardous waste produced in Minnesota to justify building this facility (JUST-FAC); whether the facility was necessary for the state of Minnesota to meet its long-term goals for a clean environment (FNECESS); and whether the state should continue looking for a facility now that/or if it was turned down in the respondent county (NOWFAC).

Respondents' general trust in government (TRUST) was measured using a series of questions about how much respondents trusted the state government to make good decisions on a variety of policy issues. The issues were tax policy (TAX), environmental issues (ENV), education (ED), agriculture (FRM), and welfare policy (WLF).

The other latent concepts included in the structural equation (i.e., TRUST-TECH, FACILITY, and NEAR TWINS) were assumed to be directly measured by the survey questions. Therefore no measurement model was specified for these latent concepts.[35]

The estimates of the measurement part of the model for Koochiching County are in Figure 4.1. The reported coefficients are from the completely standardized solution provided by LISREL 7.[36] The completely standardized solution gives beta estimates when both observed and latent variables are standardized to have a mean of zero and a variance of one. This standardization permits examination of the relative impact of each of the independent variables on the dependent variables.

The measurement model indicates that the observed variables are generally strongly related to the latent concepts. For the RISK factor all of the variables have high loadings on the latent variables. The strong loading of the variable representing people's views of the money the state was offering (MONEY) on the RISK factor indicates that those who thought that the money was adequate compensation also perceived little risk. Those who perceived a lot of risk did not feel that the money was worth the risk they perceived. The reliability of the RISK factor was quite high, .87.

The indicators for TRUST and NEED also proved to be reliable measures. The loadings for the TRUST factor were generally high. The strongest loading was for trust on environmental issues. The reliability for the TRUST factor was .90, indicating that together these observed variables were strongly related to the latent variable. Likewise for the NEED factor, the loadings of the observed variables on the latent variable were quite high. The reliability for this variable was .90.

The structural model for Koochiching County (Table 4.2) tests how well citizens' evaluation of the facility (FACILITY) is explained by the latent factors for risk assessment (RISK), trust in the state on technical issues (TRUST-TECH), belief that the facility should be built closer to the metropolitan area (NEAR TWINS), need for the facility (NEED), and general trust in the state government (TRUST). Through this relatively unrestricted model we can examine the importance of these factors in explaining citizens' attitudes and gain some understanding whether, on average, all of these are important in their evaluations.

However, the full structural model also estimates the relationships among several of the other latent factors in the model. RISK is assumed to be affected by citizens' trust in the government over technical issues (TRUST-TECH) and their views about whether the facility was necessary (NEED). In the model, opinions about trust in the state on technical issues (TRUST-TECH) are explained by peoples' perceptions about the need for the facility (NEED) and their general trust in state government on policy issues (TRUST). Respondents' attitudes about whether the facility should be near the Twin Cities (NEAR TWINS) are specified as a function of their perceptions of risk, their trust in the state on technical issues, their perceptions about the need for the facility, and their general trust in the state to make

Table 4.2 Structural Equations—Koochiching Survey

| | | | |
|---|---|---|---|
| FACILITY = (−.89)* RISK | + (.05)* TRUST-TECH | + (.035)* (NEAR TWINS) | + (.016)* TRUST |
| (−20.0) | (.62) | (.45) | (.21) |

| | | |
|---|---|---|
| RISK = (.032)* TRUST-TECH | + (−.77)* NEED | + (−.01)* TRUST |
| (.45) | (−11.1) | (−.23) |

| | |
|---|---|
| TRUST-TECH = (.26)* NEED | + (.33)* TRUST |
| (4.4) | (5.5) |

| | | | |
|---|---|---|---|
| NEAR TWINS = (.55)* RISK | + (.017)* TRUST-TECH | + (.24)* NEED | + (−.01)* TRUST |
| (3.9) | (.18) | (1.5) | (−.2) |

Adjusted goodness of fit = .96.
Chi-square to degrees of freedom = 1.5.
*Numbers under coefficients are t-statistics.

good policy. Estimating these relationships simultaneously leads to more consistent estimators.

The estimates of this model reveal that perceptions about both risk and the need for the facility have an important role in citizens' evaluation of the facility. Because the two latent variables are highly correlated, −.77, they are not both included in the structural equation with FACILITY as the dependent variable. NEED was specified to have an indirect impact on FACILITY through risk assessment (RISK). RISK has a direct effect on FACILITY of −.88. The magnitude of the coefficient indicates that NEED has an important indirect effect on FACILITY of .60.[37] Together these variables overwhelm the other factors in the model and account for nearly all of the variance in FACILITY. The other independent variables have both low standardized beta coefficients and a nonsignificant t-test, indicating that they have little impact on the dependent variables.

The lack of a significant relationship between NEAR TWINS and FACILITY has important substantive implications. If citizens were simply operating from a Nimby perspective, we would expect a very strong relationship between evaluations of the facility and opinions about where the facility should be built. The fact that there is not a significant relationship draws into question claims that citizens were merely operating from a Nimby perspective. To investigate this issue further, the survey data were cross-tabulated, and they showed that even among supporters of the facility there was considerable support for siting the facility near the Twin Cities if it was not to be sited in their county. The finding in some ways vindicates opponents of the facility. People not fearful of the facility and willing to have it in their communities also saw the benefits of locating it near the Twin Cities. This suggests that people could oppose the facility in their community for reasons other than fear and emotionalism.

Citizens' feelings that the facility should be built closer to the Twin Cities were significantly influenced by their perception of risk and need. The higher their perception of risk, the more they felt that the facility should be built near the Twin Cities. This is an important finding in the context of siting decisions because it suggests that by lowering people's perception of risk or increasing their perception of need, they might look more favorably on the facility.

Most attempts to overcome citizen opposition have focused on reducing citizen's perception of risk, as the WMB attempted to do in Minnesota. However, Alberta's successful siting effort was designed to increase citizens' perception of need by looking broadly at the province's waste generation and giving citizens a sense that disposal was just one piece of a comprehensive plan for managing waste. (This will be discussed in greater depth in Chapter 5.)

There are some other important significant relationships in the structural equation analysis. General trust in government has a positive and significant impact on citizens' trust on technical issues. In other words, those citizens who generally trust government to make good policy choices do not evaluate the state government in radically different ways on more technical issues like hazardous waste policy. However, the coefficient of .32 indicates that trust on technical issues is not fully explained by general trust. The fact that neither of these factors had a significant relationship with citizens' evaluation of the facility indicates that this trust did not translate into support for the facility.

The overall fit of the model is quite good. The coefficient of determination is .68, indicating that much of the variance in the endogenous variables was explained by other variables in the model. The adjusted goodness-of-fit index is .96, and the chi-square–to–degrees of freedom ratio is 1.5. Both of these measures provide further evidence of a good model (Bollen 1989).

The measurement model for the Red Lake survey is in Figure 4.2, and the structural model is presented in Table 4.3. The results are nearly identical to those from the Koochiching survey and will not therefore be re-

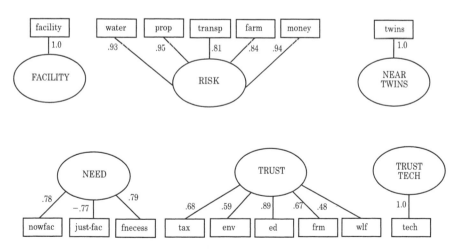

*Figure 4.2* Measurement Model for Red Lake County

*Table 4.3* Structural Equations—Red Lake Survey

| | | | | |
|---|---|---|---|---|
| FACILITY = | $(-.88)$*RISK + | $(.06)$*TRUST-TECH + | $(-.05)$*(NEAR TWINS) + | $(.056)$*TRUST |
| | $(-9.7)$ | $(.65)$ | $(-.5)$ | $(.80)$ |

RISK = $(.10)$*TRUST-TECH + $(-.99)$*NEED + $(-.003)$*TRUST
$\qquad\quad$ $(.81)$ $\qquad\qquad$ $(-7.5)$ $\qquad\quad$ $(-.05)$

TRUST-TECH = $(-.2)$*NEED + $(.44)$*TRUST
$\qquad\qquad\quad$ $(11.8)$ $\qquad$ $(4.3)$

NEAR TWINS = $(-.16)$*RISK + $(.44)$*TRUST-TECH + $(-.99)$*NEED + $(.10)$*TRUST
$\qquad\qquad\qquad$ $(-.25)$ $\qquad\quad$ $(1.5)$ $\qquad\qquad$ $(-1.4)$ $\qquad\quad$ $(-1.0)$

Adjusted goodness of fit = .99.
Chi-square to degrees of freedom = .4.
*Numbers under coefficients are t-statistics.

interpreted here. The only minor difference between the two models is the sign change in the FACILITY equation for the NEAR TWINS coefficient. Since the coefficient is not significant, the change in sign is of little substantive importance. The similarity of the two surveys' results does indicate, however, that the model is robust. Despite the different settings for the two surveys, people in the counties thought about the proposed facility in strikingly similar ways.

In the final model presented here demographic variables, like income and education, are not included. A restricted model in which these variables were more likely to have a significant impact was estimated, and it was clear that demographic characteristics did not help explain citizens' opinions about the hazardous waste facility. In addition, in a simple bivariate analysis, opinion within the counties did not appear to fall along the demographic lines that one would expect given some of the existing literature on the trade-off between environmental and economic concerns.

The survey results indicate slightly stronger support among lower-income groups, but the magnitude of the differences is small. (In Table 4.4 the cross-tabulation of income and support for the facility shows no significant relationship for Koochiching, but it does in Red Lake.) Typically those with high income and high education are thought to be stronger environmentalists than those without (on toxics, see Hamilton 1985).[38] At the same time, lower education levels seem to have a minimal impact (see Table 4.5). This is an important substantive finding because it suggests that the typical class cleavages that arise in other policy settings like welfare and tax policy break

Table 4.4 Percentage of Respondents Who Supported the Facility
by Income Categories

| | Percent Who Support the Facility | |
| Income | Koochiching | Red Lake* |
| --- | --- | --- |
| Less than $15,000 | 88.2% | 81.9% |
| $15,000–29,999 | 77.5 | 62.4 |
| $30,000–49,999 | 78.0 | 66.7 |
| $50,000 and above | 68.8 | 55.6 |

*Chi-square statistic is significant ($p < .05$).

down with regard to some environmental issues. In addition, it challenges the state government to come up with an inducement package that will appeal to citizens regardless of their socioeconomic position.

Another demographic factor that one might expect to influence citizens' evaluation of a facility is their proximity to the facility. In Koochiching the facility was going to be located near the town of Northome, at the southern end of the county. The town council of Northome had agreed to be the host for the facility because it, in particular, was suffering economically. Despite these economic problems, there was significant opposition to the facility from some of the residents of the town and in the unincorporated townships surrounding it. We might expect therefore that those closest to the facility would be more likely to approve of it, since the greatest economic benefits might go to the Northome community. On the other hand, significant support might come from those living farthest away from the site, since they could benefit from the economic package the state was offering while incurring little of the physical risk from the facility. (Dan Joyce, a member of the

Table 4.5 Percentage of Respondents Who Supported the Facility
by Educational Categories

| | Percent Who Support the Facility | |
| Education | Koochiching | Red Lake |
| --- | --- | --- |
| Some high school | 82.8% | 76.8% |
| High school graduate | 78.5 | 74.1 |
| Vocational training | 85.4 | 73.2 |
| Some college | 79.6 | 67.5 |
| College degree | 81.4 | 51.7 |
| Graduate school | 70.6 | 70.0 |

Koochiching advisory council, raised this issue, saying that he recognized that Northome would be assuming most of the risk while the rest of the county stood to benefit.)

A regression analysis was conducted to see whether those living near the proposed facility were more opposed to its construction than those living farther away from it. The results of the analysis showed no significant relationship between distance from the facility and respondents' evaluation of the facility. This finding does provide some evidence that citizens were not merely thinking about the issue through a classic Nimby perspective. If respondents simply used a Nimby framework to assess the issue, we would expect those closest to the facility to be the most fearful, but this is not what the distance analysis showed. (In Red Lake it was not clear at the time of the survey where the facility would be located if it was accepted by the citizens, so a distance analysis could not be conducted.)

## Summary of Citizens' Perceptions

Despite the variety of factors thought to be influencing citizens' evaluation of the Minnesota hazardous waste facility, this analysis reveals that only a few of these were at the center of their decision-making. Assessments of risk and evaluations of need were the overriding forces in citizens' thinking about this issue. The widespread belief that the facility posed some risk to county residents accounts for much of citizens' opposition. Citizens also remained skeptical that this facility was necessary for Minnesota to protect its environment, and they were therefore reluctant to accept it.

In addition, the belief that the facility should be built closer to the Twin Cities was broadly held. Even those who supported building the facility in their county wanted to see it built nearer the Twin Cities if the state decided to continue looking for a site. It is not too surprising that risk assessment, evaluation of need, and feelings that the facility should be built closer to the Twin Cities would have an important impact on citizens' overall evaluation of the facility. What is surprising, however, is that demographic factors and trust in the government had little impact on citizens' evaluations. Neither income nor education had any significant influence on their attitudes toward the facility. This finding was consistent in a variety of estimates, from a simple bivariate analysis to a more complex covariance structure model.

Both general trust in government on issues like tax policy, education, agriculture, welfare policy, and environmental policy, as well as trust on more technical issues like hazardous waste policy, had no significant impact on citizens' evaluation of the facility. Therefore, even though the state might be able to establish trust in some policy areas, this trust will not necessarily extend to issues like the siting of a hazardous waste facility. The failure of demographic factors and trust in government to have a significant impact on citizens' evaluation of the facility reinforces the claim that siting issues cut across traditional socioeconomic cleavages and general perceptions of government. Issues like hazardous waste siting create new challenges to government since traditional political concerns may not apply.

In addition, this analysis of Minnesota's hazardous waste policy and citizens' attitudes toward the state's proposals did provide important information about why this siting deadlock occurred and is replicated across the country. The survey analysis demonstrates a close connection between citizens' perception of risk and their perception of need: the greater citizens' perception of need, the less their perception of risk. Citizens, unlike state officials, are reluctant to trust the technology used in hazardous waste disposal and fail to see the need for the facility when alternatives like waste reduction and reclamation have not been fully developed.

However, this finding that perceptions of risk and need are closely related holds some promise for overcoming the deadlock that has generally plagued hazardous waste siting efforts. It suggests that by making citizens aware of the need for a facility, they will be more likely to accept the risk. This is consistent with more general studies of risk perception, in which the evidence shows that people are more willing to accept risk if they perceive that risk as necessary (Slovic et al. 1982). For example, state officials and supporters of the facility kept telling citizens that tanker trucks carrying gasoline down the highways were a greater threat to them than transporting hazardous waste. However, citizens knew they needed the gasoline to maintain their economy and lifestyle, but they did not perceive that they needed a hazardous waste disposal facility in their community.

## Conclusion

This examination of citizens' and state officials' perceptions of hazardous waste problems and solutions supports the argument made by advocates of substantive democracy—namely, citizens must be included in policymaking for purposes of both legitimation and problem-solving. As this case shows, citizen involvement is required for legitimation purposes, because so much of the decision-making on issues like hazardous waste is centered on normative judgments and these issues cannot be resolved through the application of expert knowledge.

Citizens in both Red Lake and Koochiching Counties generally reacted negatively to building the hazardous waste facility in their communities. On the whole, their normative judgments were that the facility was a risk to the community through groundwater contamination, possible spills during transportation of the waste, and decline in property values. At the same time, many citizens felt the facility should more appropriately be sited near the source of production.

These beliefs are in stark contrast to the thinking of state officials. They believed that the facility was necessary for Minnesota to address its own waste problems and that the plans they developed were more than adequate to protect citizens and the environment from damage by the treatment and transport of hazardous waste. These differences in perceived risk from the facility echo the findings at the national level, in which citizens and EPA officials exhibited different perceptions of risk.[39] In addition, state officials remained steadfast in their belief that this was not simply a concern for the industrialized urban areas. They contended that all citizens of the state had an equal responsibility to work together to find solutions to environmental problems, and they were reluctant to accept the normative argument advanced by residents of Koochiching and Red Lake Counties that the facility should be sited near the source of production.

These differences in normative judgments cannot necessarily be resolved through an appeal to "the facts" at hand. For state officials, the central normative question was how to deal with Minnesota's waste and manage the state's waste stream into the future. For citizens, the normative issues were who should bear the risk and what was fair. If a democratic government is to remain legitimate in the eyes of its citizens, these normative differences cannot be resolved through technical decision-making but must be settled through political deliberation.

## Notes

1. Donald Kennedy, former President of Stanford University, could be included in this list of skeptics of citizen participation on important public matters. He argues, "a new and corrosive popular mistrust of scientists and their work [is generating] political

constraints that are already cutting into the growth of our science, cutting into the capacity to help us resolve our . . . problems" (as quoted in Piller 1991, 4).

William Ophuls (1977, 1992) provides a strong argument for guardianship and technocracy as the only way to avert an ecological disaster. In the topic of regulation of risks, Breyer (1993) argues for a technocratic solution. See also Schumpeter (1947) and Berelson (1952) for skeptical accounts of citizen participation. For an overview of the debate, see Cronin (1989, Chapters 1 to 3) and Fishkin (1995, Chapter 2).

2. As evidence of the need to rely on experts on technical issues, critics of citizen participation point to the failure of the general public to demonstrate rudimentary scientific literacy. A public opinion survey conducted in 1985 by the Northern Illinois University Public Opinion Laboratory shows that "only one-third of Americans say they clearly understand what a molecule is, though the term is used freely by the press and in advertising. Five out of six Americans do not understand genetic engineering. Less than one-third of adults say they have a clear knowledge of what radiation is" (Miller 1987, 26).

3. Dahl in particular argues that there is no "objective" general interest for policy experts to discover. What is best for a community is what its members collectively decide through open and informed deliberation (Dahl 1989, 70–74).

4. Kunreuther and Slovic (1996) argue that experts tend to think of risk as objective and quantifiable, but that citizens have a conception of risk that is qualitative and "incorporates considerations such as uncertainty, dread, catastrophic potential, controllability, equity, [and] risk to future generations" (121).

5. "Polls Show Contrasts in How Public and E.P.A. View Environment," *New York Times,* 22 March 1989.

6. Ibid.

Feldman and Hanahan (1999) recently completed a study that uses citizens' perception of risk to help set environmental priorities.

7. Ideally one would like to have similar survey instruments to compare citizens' and state officials' attitudes toward hazardous waste issues. However, due to the small number of state officials who actually dealt with this issue, meaningful comparisons between citizens and state officials using survey results was not possible. Because of this, I will draw on interview materials to characterize expert opinion and then compare these findings with interviews and survey material gathered from citizens.

8. See Appendix A for details of the survey.

9. Hunter and Leyden (1995) attempt to explain attitudes toward a hazardous waste incinerator in West Virginia using similar factors, like the citizens' attitudes regarding the impact of the facility on property rights, risk assessment, knowledge about the facility, etc.

10. Kent Portney (1991, 1988), using survey data, and Michael Elliot (1984), using an experimental setting, find that risk is the most important factor in citizens' opposition to having a facility near them.

11. Velma Oakland, interview with author, Red Lake Falls, Minnesota, 9 April 1990.

12. According to the National Weather Service, the average annual snowfall is 63 inches in Koochiching County and 46.4 inches in Red Lake County. The average winter high is 15.9° in Koochiching and 18.0° in Red Lake.

13. Written response to survey, Koochiching County.

14. Ken Stabler, Facility Development Manager, Minnesota Waste Management Board, interview with author, St. Paul, Minnesota, 20 June 1990.

15. Gene Ulring, County Engineer of Red Lake County, interview with author, Red Lake Falls, Minnesota, 9 April 1990.

16. Williams and Matheny (1995) explicitly address the need to bring these disparate approaches together in their discussion of the dialogic model.

17. The argument made by both people in business and state decision-makers was that putting the waste in the safest possible facility would help hedge against future liability since such a facility would be less likely to have an accident or leak.

18. Neil Miller, Public Affairs Officer for the Minnesota Waste Management Board, interview with author, St. Paul, Minnesota, 29 April 1990.

19. These same questions were not asked in the Koochiching survey due to limited space.

20. For example, in his study of the Massachusetts hazardous waste siting attempt, Portney (1991, 62) finds deep distrust of state, local, and federal officials on the siting issue.

21. Dan Joyce, member of the Koochiching County advisory council, interview with author, Littlefork, Minnesota, 27 September 1989.

22. "Northome Commissioner Talks about His Role," *Clipper Viewpoint,* 28 December 1988, 1.

23. Suspicion of government officials and their exercise of power has long been part of American political culture, from the time of the founding to the 19th-century politics observed by Tocqueville, to the skepticism of (and at times hostility toward) government decision-making evident in contemporary politics.

24. Some opponents argued that they would be willing to accept such a facility if they received as compensation jobs that would substantially improve their community's economy. This view appeared not to have been widely held since most respondents said that they would be unwilling to accept a facility even if more jobs were brought into the county.

25. Written response to survey, Koochiching County.

26. Gene Ulring, County Engineer of Red Lake County, interview with author, Red Lake Falls, Minnesota, 9 April 1990.

27. These same questions were not asked in the Koochiching survey due to limited space.

28. Russ Susag, Environmental Officer 3M Corporation, interview with author, St. Paul, Minnesota, 30 June 1990.

29. Susan Boyle, resident of Koochiching County, interview with author, International Falls, Minnesota, 26 September 1989.

30. Jean Moser, member of the Red Lake County advisory council, interview with author, Red Lake Falls, Minnesota, 10 April 1990.

31. Jody Gross, member of the Northland Concerned Citizens, interview with author, Northome, Minnesota, 28 September 1989.

32. Neil Miller, Public Affairs Officer, Minnesota Waste Management Board, interview with author, St. Paul, Minnesota, 29 April 1990.

33. Ibid.

34. In more extensive studies of economic incentives and hazardous waste siting, Portney (1991, 1988) and Elliot (1984) also find that citizens are not likely to view facilities more favorably when offered monetary incentives.

35. In other words, the factor loading for the indicator on the latent variable was set to one.

36. Appendix C describes the appropriate transformations to the covariance matrix to address the issue of a small number of response categories in the survey questions.

37. Because of the closeness of these two concepts the analysis was also done specifying a RISK-NEED factor as a second-order factor analysis. The RISK-NEED factor was then used as an independent variable in the structural equation for FACILITY. Both RISK and NEED were highly related to the RISK-NEED factor, confirming their similarity in citizens' evaluation of the facility. The substantive interpretation of this model replicated the one described here. Because the model without the second-order factor was substantively the same and simpler to interpret, it was chosen for presentation in this chapter.

38. However, on general attitudes toward the environment, researchers find that ideological factors are more important than socioeconomic factors (Samdahl and Robertson 1989).

39. "Polls Show Contrasts in How Public and E.P.A. View Environment," *New York Times,* 22 March 1989; Greenberg (1984).

# CHAPTER 5

# Democratic Governance and Policymaking

Thinking, in its . . . non-specialized sense as a natural need of human life . . . is not a prerogative of the few but an ever-present faculty in everybody; by the same token, inability to think is not a failing of the many who lack brain power but an ever-present possibility for everybody—scientists, scholars, and other specialists in mental enterprises not excluded.

Hannah Arendt
*The Life of the Mind*

The Nimby syndrome evokes powerful images of policymaking in peril—irrational and parochial citizens control decisions on hazardous waste disposal and regularly prevent the construction of disposal facilities that are necessary for the safe management of the nation's waste. Public officials also contribute to the Nimby syndrome because they lack the political will to confront citizens and make difficult choices. Implicit in the language and images of the Nimby syndrome is a technocratic view of good policymaking. In this view our collective interests are best served through rational deliberation among policy experts who possess the knowledge and objectivity to choose the optimal strategy for hazardous waste disposal. Democratic deliberation and political conflict only contribute to our inability to solve difficult problems.

This perspective does have some appeal in a political context in which citizens' knowledge of and interest in politics is generally thought to be low and political officials are seen as too beholden to public opinion (Inhaber 1998). However, the detailed look into Minnesota's hazardous waste policy presented here demonstrates the ways in which the Nimby view of policymaking is flawed. In this chapter I summarize policymaking in Minnesota and argue that rather than being powerful, as the Nimby syndrome implies, citizens had limited political resources and struggled to control the process. In addition, state officials did not simply concede control of policymaking once citizen opposition arose. Instead, they marshaled significant state resources to mold public opinion and site the stabilization and containment facility. Rather than impeding good policymaking, this political conflict between citizens and policy experts helped the state avoid investment in an unnecessary and expensive facility and ultimately led to an effective strategy for managing the state's waste.

## Control of Policymaking

Minnesota's hazardous waste decision-making shows the difficult and protracted journey that citizens must make to influence policy on technical issues like the siting of hazardous waste facilities. This was evident early in the policymaking process, when citizens were not involved in the discussions in the 1980s about the general direction that the state's hazardous waste policy would take. They did not play a central role in deciding if disposal would be above- or below-ground, if the state would use its powers of eminent domain to site the facility, if site selection would be based on a scientific evaluation of geological characteristics, and if all counties in the state would be potential hosts of the facility or only those who were the primary producers of hazardous waste. These decisions were made primarily through negotiations among urban-based elite environmental groups, businesses who produced this waste, and personnel of the Waste Management Board. The evidence from the initial attempt by the Minnesota legislature to address the state's hazardous waste problems through the Waste Management Act and the formation of the Waste Management Board attests to the important influence of elite groups on policy formation and the limited impact that the opinions of unorganized citizens can play at this formative stage of the process.

Once these important decisions were made and the parameters of the debate set, citizens had some access to decision-making through the hearings the state conducted. The state's motivations for these hearings were complex. State officials learned from their experience in trying to site the EPA-sponsored facility that the public could not be completely cut out of the siting process. Citizen participation would legitimize the decision and increase the likelihood that they would accept the facility. The state hoped that its efforts to educate the public through these statewide hearings would increase awareness of the hazardous waste problem but also lead citizens to think about the problem in the same way that state officials did. In other words, state officials did not take public opinion as fixed, but tried to alter it in a way that would coincide with their own policy preferences. Importantly, there is no evidence that citizens were included with the expectation that their involvement would improve the decision-making process.

However, this case also demonstrates how citizens can overcome these attempts by policy experts to control the process. In the first siting attempt under the Waste Management Act (1980–1984) policymaking unfolded in a way consistent with McCubbins and Schwartz's "fire alarm" model of political control (see Chapter 2). Constituents from the districts that were potential sites for the hazardous waste landfill aired their objections to their legislators and managed to cast enough doubt that a moratorium was imposed. They raised critical questions about the forecasted amounts of waste that state officials used to justify the facility, the safety of landfill disposal, and the likelihood that out-of-state landfills would be closed. Therefore, despite the obvious support of important business and environmental groups to push ahead with the landfill disposal siting, citizens ultimately disrupted the elite negotiations and rebuffed the state's efforts to site a landfill using eminent domain.

Ironically, the political stalemate that developed between influential groups who pushed for a disposal site and citizens who resisted it provided the opportunity for the WMB to develop greater autonomy in hazardous waste decision-making. Because citizen opposition prompted a veto of the solution preferred by elite interest groups, the WMB had greater latitude to develop a solution that it felt would best serve Minnesota's needs. Rather than choose between the preferences of elite interest groups or citizens WMB officials relied on their technical evaluations and pushed for the stabilization and containment facility—the solution they thought would provide safe and reliable disposal capacity for Minnesota into the future.

As a result of the stalemate citizens faced a different set of obstacles in their effort to control policy in the second stage of the process (1986–1990).

The WMB developed some autonomy in the formulation of hazardous waste policy, but it had to rely on the state's noncoercive capacity to gain acceptance of the facility from Minnesota counties. The Waste Management Board, with the tentative support of the legislature, marshaled its resources and expertise to design a voluntary siting strategy, one they hoped would minimize public opposition and ensure successful siting of the new stabilization and containment facility.

As part of the voluntary siting process the state implemented a public relations campaign so that county residents would view the facility more favorably. To this end, they planned their interactions with the media to ensure that the project would be presented positively and county residents would get the "facts." The WMB also tried to educate the public by conducting seminars and small group meetings and organizing tours of hazardous waste facilities in other areas. This use of state money and expertise created a disparity between opponents and the state since the WMB had substantial resources at its disposal and could more easily communicate its message. In an attempt to take the moral high ground in the debate state officials argued that opponents of the facility were motivated by selfishness and parochialism and were preventing the state as a whole from achieving its collective well-being. As a final attempt to gain public support in Koochiching County the WMB and members of the legislature contemplated a direct-mail campaign immediately before the proposed referendum to ensure that people received the information at an opportune time and that the opposition would not have a chance to rebut.

Ultimately, despite drawing on its noncoercive capacities, the state failed to secure a site through the voluntary process. Thus, even in the face of substantial pressures from the state, citizens were able to exert some measure of control over hazardous waste policy. The fact that this control could occur in Minnesota is significant because the Minnesota state government had an experienced agency and substantial resources upon which to draw. The state spent $10 million to study its hazardous waste problems and to inform and persuade its citizens of the importance and safety of a stabilization and containment facility.

However, it is important to recognize that the control that citizens were able to exert after gaining access to the decision-making process was primarily oppositional. They were able to prevent the state from achieving its objectives, thus curbing its capacity without really curtailing its autonomy. Only after citizens twice vetoed the state's siting efforts did state officials truly emphasize recycling, reclamation, and reduction over disposal as a policy goal.

This study shows the difficult and persistent effort that citizens must make to influence policymaking. Rather than finding state officials who were open to their opinions, citizens encountered policymakers who were often skeptical of their views and questioned their ability to make good policy choices. Thus policymakers do not simply respond mechanically to public opinion, and rather than taking citizens' views as fixed, state officials use their financial, technological, and informational resources and work to alter the preferences of citizens so that they are consistent with their own preferences.

The implications of the state's attempt to gain the consent of citizens are important for understanding contemporary policymaking. Metaphors of a "cash register state" are now anachronistic. Modern states do not merely measure the pressures they are receiving and decide in favor of the group or coalition of groups mounting the most successful campaigns. Also, despite claims that decision-makers are too beholden to public opinion, the evidence here shows that they are often reluctant to follow opinion and even take some pride in resisting it. Moreover, states use their resources to develop their own policy initiatives and to alter societal preferences to support their plans. It is because of the development of the administrative state, with its technical and financial resources, that citizens who want to influence policy decisions must not only press their preferences upon decision-makers, but must also withstand overt efforts by the state to alter their perceptions of the problem.

The state's ability to use its resources in this way sheds a different light on waste siting and the Nimby syndrome. Rather than being concerned that policymaking is firmly in the hands of citizens who use their power to disrupt well-formulated policy, we should worry about state officials' capacity to exercise control over these citizens' opinions.

## Consequences of Citizen Involvement

The siting effort in Minnesota also provides important evidence of the positive impact that citizens can have on policymaking and of the problems associated with reliance on expert decision-makers. This is obviously a controversial claim in the context of hazardous waste policy, about which some have argued that citizen opposition to state policy initiatives is evidence that the democracy has become counterproductive to making "good" public policy rather than being essential to it.[1] As John Kemeny, who chaired the presidential commission that reviewed the Three Mile Island accident, said, "Jeffersonian democracy cannot work in the year 1980. The world has become too complex."[2] Policymakers in Minnesota certainly developed the sense that they understood the problems the state confronted at the time and those it would face in the future better than citizens did. They were confident that the facility was in Minnesota's best interest and that those who opposed the facility suffered from naïveté and narrow self-interest.

However, and perhaps most important, this case demonstrates the positive impact that citizens had on Minnesota's hazardous waste decisions and the ways in which citizens can contribute to good policymaking more generally. In challenging state decision-makers over the need for a facility, citizens used the WMB's own estimates to show that the amount of waste produced in Minnesota cast doubt on the need for a facility. In addition, calculations of profitability revealed that the facility was only marginally economically viable because stabilization and containment is costlier than landfill disposal. It was not clear that the state could run this facility at capacity without 3M participating, since the waste from 3M's incinerator constituted more than 25 percent of the inorganic waste produced in the state. However, because 3M has facilities around the country it was not likely to be locked out of landfills in other states and would only use the facility if Minnesota could offer a price that was competitive with current rates. Finally, calculations of profitability would only have held up if the level of waste remained relatively constant over the subsequent twenty years and future recycling and reclamation programs did not significantly reduce the amount of waste produced. If the waste stream were reduced, the facility could only be viable if the price of disposal rose significantly across the country.

These contributions that citizens made to Minnesota's hazardous waste policy appear even more important when stated in the form of a counterfactual argument. In the first phase of the siting effort (1980–1984), without the mobilization of citizens, the state would have sited a landfill and locked the state into disposal technology that it subsequently decided to abandon in favor of stabilization and containment disposal. It would have made this decision based on inflated estimates of the amount of hazardous waste in Minnesota, a fact the WMB itself demonstrated in its later (1988) assessment of need. In addition, citizen opposition prevented the state from experimenting with an unproven technology—bedrock disposal of hazardous waste. In the second phase of the siting effort citizens prevented the state from building a facility that was in many ways ill-suited to Minnesota's hazardous waste needs. The facility would have provided disincentives for recycling and reclamation; it would have required importing waste from other states to meet break-even costs; and the major producer of hazardous waste in the state had publicly stated it would not use the facility at the price the state used in its cost-effectiveness calculations. Through their opposition, and ultimately their veto of the facility, citizens prevented the state from investing in a facility that was of questionable need, a potential drain on state resources, and a disincentive to recycling, reclamation, and reduction of waste.

The contribution of citizens to policymaking is also readily apparent through an examination of the state's reformulation of its hazardous waste policy once siting the facility seemed doomed. In the following pages I describe the shift in policymaking that began after a decade of citizen opposition to siting a disposal facility and outline the successful programs that may not have been vigorously pursued otherwise.

At the beginning of the 1990 legislative session the Toxic Pollution Prevention Act (TPPA) was passed with the endorsement of legislators active on environmental issues, environmental groups, and some key businesses like 3M.[3] The bill brought together those interested in industrial hazardous waste, household hazardous waste, toxic chemical releases, and a variety of other pollution issues. For those working on industrial hazardous waste issues, the bill offered an opportunity to restructure the state's hazardous waste strategy at a time when there were lingering doubts that the stabilization and containment facility was economically viable and that Red Lake County would approve the contract.

One key legislator who played a significant role in the development of the state's waste policy reported that by 1990 there was very little hope that citizens would approve the facility in the referendum, and thus state officials felt that they needed to increase the state's pollution reduction efforts to manage waste effectively.[4] This point was also confirmed in the 1992 Capacity Assurance Plan that the state sent to the EPA. In updating the EPA on the status of the facility the WMB reported:

A referendum on the issue of whether to host the facility was defeated in the lone remaining county in November 1990. Minnesota is presently reexamining the extent of its need for such a facility and investigating other options such as targeted pollution prevention activities to landfill users and expanding existing facilities to include stabilization.[5]

According to state officials, "this law [the TPPA] established a new emphasis in environmental policy: preventing pollution at the source in ways that minimize the transfer of pollutants from one environmental medium to another (e. g., from water to air)."[6] This new legislation greatly expanded the Minnesota Technical Assistance Program, which from 1984 to 1989 provided technical and financial assistance to small businesses to help them reduce their waste generation. In its 1992 Capacity Assurance Plan the WMB noted that "the passage of the TPPA in 1990 expanded the program into multimedia pollution prevention assistance for all 'persons who use, generate, or release, toxic pollutants, hazardous substances, or hazardous waste' (Minn. Stat. 115D. 03, subd. 5)."[7] In other words, the program was now intended to help large waste generators manage their waste to reduce the state's overall level of pollution.

Also, under this new legislative initiative the state requires firms to pay fees for each chemical they release ($150 per chemical released) and a tonnage fee ($500 for facilities releasing less than 25,000 pounds and two cents per pound for facilities that release more than 25,000 pounds). The payment is capped at $30,000 per plant. These fees generated approximately $1 million per year from 1993 through 1997.[8] The fines go into a fund that will help companies design new strategies for reducing their waste. In addition, waste generators who are required to file a Toxic Chemical Release Inventory under Section 313 of the federal Emergency Planning and Community Right-to-Know Act must develop a pollution prevention plan that describes the steps they will take to reduce waste and to report their progress to the Minnesota Pollution Control Agency.

The TPPA also established the Governor's Award for Excellence in Pollution Prevention to recognize the waste reduction efforts of Minnesota generators and expanded the WMB's grant program to assist businesses in those efforts. Thus state policy gives waste generators an incentive to find methods to reduce or eliminate their waste and provides technical and financial assistance to help them meet those goals.

In addition to the Toxic Pollution Prevention Act, the legislature approved several amendments to the Waste Management Act in 1992 and 1993 which were intended to reduce the amount of pollution produced in the state. These amendments included additional labeling requirements for hazardous materials in some consumer products, restrictions on the disposal of antifreeze and other fluids from automobiles, and additional limits on the use of heavy metals like lead, cadmium, and mercury in inks, dyes, and paints used or sold in the state. The state legislature also reorganized and changed the name of the Office of Waste Management to the Office of Environmental Assistance. This change reflected the renewed commitment of the state to pollution reduction. The mission of this new agency was to provide technical assistance to businesses to assist their waste reduction efforts and to better educate industry and the public about waste issues. The agency no longer used its financial and staff resources to site a disposal facility in Minnesota.

According to policymakers, several factors came together and prompted the state to renew its effort at waste minimization. First, as noted earlier, many policymakers doubted that the state could successfully site the stabilization and containment facility. In addition, in the early 1990s it became evident to policymakers that the widespread concern about the lack of disposal capacity nationwide was unwarranted. Partly due to the increased costs of landfill disposal and the increased regulation of disposal practices, businesses recognized that they had incentives to reduce the amount of waste that they produced or to dispose of it on-site to avoid the costs of disposal (Gerrard 1994; Szasz 1994).[9] Therefore predictions in the early 1980s about landfills reaching their capacity were wrong, and this meant that Minnesota businesses who needed to dispose of waste were able to continue to ship their waste out of state (although they faced increasing costs).

As programs like MnTap and grants from the Office of Environmental Assistance helped Minnesota businesses minimize the amount of waste going to landfills (despite an average annual growth rate of 5 percent in the state's economy from 1990 to 1994), they further reduced the need for the state to provide its own disposal facility. The amount of waste shipped to out-of-state landfills reached its peak in 1990 at 12,414 tons, but from 1992 to 1996 the amount Minnesota businesses shipped to landfills decreased 28.7 percent.[10]

Finally, Metro Recovery Systems, the company that had planned to build a metal recovery plant in Roseville, Minnesota, in the 1980s, was purchased by US Filter. In 1988 US Filter opened Minnesota's first major hazardous waste treatment facility and could provide metal recovery and aqueous treatment services to hazardous waste generators. From 1994 to 1996 the US Filter facility processed approximately 20,000 tons of metals and other inorganic waste.[11] Because this facility gave the state the means to process some of its waste in the Twin Cities metro area, it helped align the state's management strategy with the preferences of citizens in Red Lake and Koochiching Counties, who opposed the stabilization and containment facility. They consistently argued that the waste should be handled near the source of production and that those who received the economic benefits from industrial production should also take responsibility for the environmental and health risks.

In 1992 US Filter began feasibility studies to determine whether its plant could process some of Minnesota's inorganic waste that was sent out of state for disposal. If the stabilization of the waste were successful, it could be rendered nonhazardous and disposed of in the state. The Minnesota Industrial Containment Facility, a landfill disposal facility designed to handle nonhazardous industrial waste, was built in Rosemount, Minnesota, and could accept the waste residual from the US Filter plant.[12] However, the feasibility studies conducted by US Filter indicated that stabilization of the waste was not viable economically, given falling costs for disposal nationwide. If market conditions changed, the two facilities could work together to process some of Minnesota's waste.[13]

In 1990, then, after many years of citizen opposition to a disposal facility, the state began to restructure its waste management strategy so that waste minimization was the overriding concern. State officials maintained that this emphasis on waste reduction was always present but was overshadowed by the highly publicized siting effort. However, the innovations of the 1990s demonstrated that there was much more that the state could do in terms of waste reduction.

Ultimately, the decisions made in the 1990s confirmed the views of citizens who opposed the facility—namely, that it was not really needed in Minnesota if the state made a stronger commitment to waste reduction. The success of the state's programs in the 1990s demonstrates the wisdom of the citizens' position and makes charges of Nimbyism suspect. In an interview an anonymous state official further confirmed that citizen opposition was actually beneficial to the state. He conceded that the facility was only marginally economically viable in 1990 and that the continued availability of landfill disposal in other states made it unlikely that Minnesota could have profitably operated its stabilization and containment facility. He believed that the waste facility "would have gone under in five years," because "the margin was too tight."[14]

In one of its own reports published after the stabilization and containment facility had been rejected, the WMB recommended to the legislature that the state not pursue further development of a state-owned hazardous waste stabilization and containment facility in the near future. Developments related to waste supply, Capacity Assurance, access to new facilities in Canada, and the potential for private sector involvement in Minnesota reinforce the OWM's [formerly the WMB] recommendation.[15]

In the report, agency officials contend that Minnesota only generates about 10,000 tons of waste each year that needs to be sent to a landfill, and "this quantity cannot economically support a facility solely for Minnesota's waste."[16]

In the end, this analysis shows that citizen involvement in issues like hazardous waste disposal is valuable and demonstrates the benefits of citizen activism and democratic decision-making rather than their failures. Minnesota does not appear to have needed this disposal facility, and therefore it would have been a mistake on the part of state officials to invest large sums of state money and other resources into it. Thus this case suggests that we should view with suspicion claims that the development of state capacity and autonomy and the insulation of political decision-making can lead to policies that serve "the general interest." On issues like hazardous waste policy experts hold no privileged understanding of the normative or instrumental issues entailed in policymaking. At the same time, citizens are not just blinded by the Nimby syndrome but can play an important role in policymaking by challenging experts' decisions and helping in the evolution of decisions that are not merely arrived at technically.

Even when citizens are concerned about the impact of a hazardous waste facility in their own community (as citizens in Minnesota were), they can make important contributions to policymaking. Parochialism and lack of technical sophistication on the part of citizens might not be as problematic for society as the skeptics of democracy and those distressed by the Nimby syndrome suggest. As Lindblom notes:

[T]he narrow form of partisanship stirs anxieties. . . . Yet good problem solving requires responses not only to many common volitions but also to many private and segmental volitions. Good problem solving requires attention to the special volitions of each of various subgroups—children, elderly, farmers, or disabled, for example—even at a cost to other groups. (1990, 52)

Partisanship can play an important role in political debates because it sensitizes decision-makers to the needs and perspectives of a diverse populous. This conflictual engagement between partisan probing and expert decision-making is especially important on complex issues like hazardous waste siting, since errors can have widespread and calamitous consequences for the well-being of citizens and the environment. Including partisan perspectives in the debate makes decision-making more difficult because a variety of perspectives on the problem will be articulated and there is no objective, scientific standpoint from which to evaluate them. But this kind of process is likely to lead to more effective decision-making in the long run, as state officials hear and address the concerns of citizens and avoid the problems of insulated and specialized thinking.

In response to accusations of parochialism, one of the opponents of the facility in Koochiching County made a similar argument regarding the importance of including local interests in policy debates. She contended that in a democracy it was her responsibility to think about the impact of political decisions on her community. "I think of it as concentric circles. First, I look out there to my backyard, then to the county, and then to the state. But someone has to look out for my backyard. The people in Hennepin County [the Twin Cities area] aren't going to."[17] It is through the expression of multiple local concerns that we come to understand the "common good" for a political community. This view of the policymaking process is consistent with that of Dahl and Lindblom, who argue that there is no objective "common good" that exists above a polity, but that the common good is discovered through the articulation and consideration of the variety of viewpoints from those who make up a political community.[18]

Lindblom also argues that we should be suspicious of public information campaigns which attempt to get citizens to view political problems as policy experts do. Rather than purge citizens' perspective from the debate by emphasizing technical and objective criteria, political debates should give citizens' perspectives equal standing. Lindblom contends that citizens have not been "impaired" by scientific training the way that policy experts have and can therefore provide a unique and important perspective on political problems. Specialists are trained to think in a particular way, which often leads them to ignore or be ignorant of problems which may be relevant to the issue at hand but outside of their area of specialization.[19] Perhaps we should not be satisfied, but rather worried, when citizens adopt the perspective of policy experts.

It is important to recognize that the contribution that citizens can make to understanding the common good and policymaking making is not simply the result of an opportunity to participate. As Fishkin (1995) argues, the changes to political institutions that have occurred this century, like initiative and referendum and more elected offices at the state and local level, have given citizens more opportunities to participate but not necessarily to deliberate. As Williams and Matheny (1995) contend and Minnesota's experience shows, effective hazardous waste policy requires deliberation among policymakers and citizens in order for them to better understand each other and to find workable solutions.

## Minnesota Exceptionalism?

If Minnesota's experience with citizen mobilization leading to better policy can be seen as a success for democratic decision-making, it is important to consider whether this same process of democratic and expert competition can lead to better policies in other locales.[20] Two national studies of hazardous waste policy in the states suggest that Minnesota's experience is not unique.[21] As Szasz (1994) and Gerrard (1994) argue, the most significant development in this policy area in recent years is a greater concern with waste reduction and less emphasis on disposal. Szasz credits this shift in emphasis to the spread of grassroots opposition groups (what he calls "the toxics movement") across the country and to changes in federal policy that increased disposal costs, liability, and insurance premiums for waste generators. As disposal became more expensive, businesses began to look for ways to reduce their costs and turned to waste reduction.

Szasz argues that citizens contributed to the long-term term rationality of waste management through their opposition to waste disposal:

Environmentalists and scientists, government and industry, now agree that pollution prevention through source reduction is the most desirable, possibly the only workable, solution to the nation's waste problem. . . . Even if local resistance results in some increase in unsafe disposal or illegal dumping, in the short run, mass refusal produces a rational result in the long run because it is the force that is pushing society toward a less antagonistic, more sustainable relationship with nature. (Szasz 1994, 149)

In states all across the country citizens have gathered and shared information about the safety and effectiveness of waste disposal. And this nationwide opposition can be plausibly defended as an important factor in redirecting waste policy from its emphasis on waste disposal in the 1980s to a greater focus on waste reduction in the 1990s.

There are also some striking parallels between Minnesota's hazardous waste policy and those of the federal government during the 1990s, and these suggest that Minnesota's experience is not atypical. In 1990 the federal government passed its own Pollution Prevention Act which, like Minnesota's, gave greater emphasis to waste reduction. The EPA has implemented a variety of new programs to promote waste reduction, including one that gives incentives to state, regional, and local governments to develop their own waste reduction efforts (Ochsner and Chess 1996).

## An Alternative Siting Strategy—Yimby

Although it is my contention here that the struggle between democratic and technical decision-making that occurred in Minnesota was ultimately beneficial to the state, it is important to consider the ways in which partisan probing and expert decision-making could work together more deliberatively in hazardous waste management. Here I describe the Yimby (Yes, In Many Back Yards) siting strategy—sometimes referred to as "fair share siting"—and how it integrates partisan probing with more technical judgments about hazardous waste management. I then assess its virtues and limitations as a means to effective, democratic hazardous waste policymaking.

The Yimby approach to siting developed in the late 1980s and early 1990s as a response to policymakers' inability to site hazardous waste facilities.[22] Rather than tackle the siting problem directly, Yimby takes an integrated approach to hazardous waste management by looking at ways to simultaneously reduce, recycle, and dispose of waste. To facilitate integration the Yimby plan redirects the responsibility for safe management of the waste further down from the state to the local level so that communities can identify their waste problem and decide how to address it. In this approach communities cannot act in isolation because they are required to think about their waste problem in relation to nearby communities and to develop cooperative solutions when possible.

In the siting dialogue, each community would see how its proposed share of the region's new facility would fit in with all the rest; each would be participating equitably in effective management of the region's overall waste volume. Local residents would be able to see the appropriateness of those facilities proposed for their own area, as part of their basic responsibility to manage the volume of wastes equivalent to the amount generated by tax-paying and job-creating industries in their own community. (Morell 1987)

In these negotiations communities with the greatest problems are forced to put the most effort and resources into finding a solution, but all communities must contribute to waste management. These contributions can range from housing a collection and transfer station in areas with small quantities of waste, to siting a hazardous waste facility in high waste-producing areas. This strategy is designed to help overcome the possibility that poor or isolated communities would bear undue risk for hazardous waste disposal, since they are often not the major waste generators. In addition, by localizing the decision and promoting citizens' involvement from the early, problem-definition stages onward, this process allows citizens to articulate their partisan interests and for these concerns to help shape the context and direction of policies.[23]

The results from the analysis of citizen opinion in this case study of Minnesota's hazardous waste policy support the Yimby approach as a useful alternative to eminent domain or voluntary siting and compensation packages. The survey analysis reveals that citizens' perceptions of need and their perceptions of risk are highly negatively related. This suggests that when citizens believe that there is a need for something like a disposal facility or a transfer station, their perceptions of risk will shift accordingly. The Yimby plan holds some promise because it begins by asking communities to assess the problems in their area so that citizens can see the need to protect their environment from damage due to improper handling or disposal of hazardous waste. Once the immediate need is determined, appropriate solutions can be developed to ameliorate these problems.[24]

Siting strategies like Yimby have been endorsed by a number of researchers who believe that it can combine democratic principles with effective waste management. For example, with the goal of providing a more equitable distribution of risk from hazardous and nuclear waste disposal facilities, Gerrard (1994) outlines a plan for an integrated approach to waste management with significant public involvement and cooperation across state borders. In Gerrard's proposal the federal government would require regions, states, and municipalities to identify their most important waste problems and devise solutions to them. These plans would then be coordinated so that political jurisdictions could take care of their most pressing problem. For example, a state with a large radioactive waste problem would build disposal facilities and accept waste from other states with less need. In turn, states with significant amounts of hazardous waste would take responsibility for managing this waste and accept waste from other states.

Similarly, Williams and Matheny (1995) propose a dialogic model for waste management that explicitly integrates democratic decision-making. Their proposal calls for broad political, societal, and economic transformations to make the dialogue between citizens and elites more equitable and meaningful. Because of their emphasis on dialogue and participation, in their specific recommendations for hazardous waste management they see the Yimby strategy as promising. For them it is important for citizens to participate in an ongoing dialogue with policymakers over the nature of hazardous waste policy and alternatives for effective and equitable waste management. They further argue (with Barber 1984) that participation in policymaking strengthens citizens' faith and interest in politics and democratic deliberation. Therefore strategies like Yimby have societal benefits beyond the issue of hazardous waste.

The Yimby approach to waste management is designed to overcome two potential limits to democratic decision-making on hazardous waste issues. First, one common concern among policymakers is that citizens only get interested in an issue like hazardous waste when it threatens their own backyard. Thus it is difficult to motivate citizens to participate in more general debates about these issues when the costs and benefits are not personally felt.[25] Although the Yimby approach to waste management is no panacea, by creating and funding procedures for communities to design solutions to their waste problems it does provide motivation for citizens to get involved in political decision-making.

A second concern with democratic institutions is their inability to provide long-term planning. Because policymakers often respond to the demands of mobilized citizens and interest groups who frequently want short-term results, the long-term interests of unmobilized citizens and future generations are not adequately represented. The Yimby approach to siting does in some ways reduce this problem since it is designed to increase mobilization and encourage all citizens to think about the waste problem, and they or their descendants will likely have to deal with the consequences of their decisions for their community.

Despite its promise and compatibility with a model of democratic decision-making, the effectiveness of the Yimby approach has not yet been demonstrated. In California the state legislature passed the Hazardous Waste Management Act (AB 2948), which was signed by the governor in 1986. The act called for the fifty-eight counties in the state to develop a comprehensive program to manage their waste. The goal was to have all counties involved in the waste issue, not just those that produced the majority of the waste or those that might be hosts for a disposal facility. The act was based on fair-share principles, and it was hoped that a full range of waste facilities—including transfer stations, recycling centers, and disposal facilities—would be built.

Each county's plan had to be approved by the state Department of Health Services (DHS). State law gave DHS the authority to develop guidelines for approving the counties' management plans. As DHS developed these guidelines it became clear to the counties that the agency did not accept "the central role of fair share and intercounty agreements in the statute" (Morell 1996, 150). DHS believed that market forces should dictate siting decisions, and this meant that urban waste generators would once again try to build facilities in remote counties with inexpensive land. In his evaluation of California's implementation of the Hazardous Waste Management Act, Morell (1996) concludes:

> From the counties' perspective, their whole agreement with the state over the content of the act had been betrayed. . . . Of course, by changing the fundamental dynamics of the siting process, no one won. DHS's revisions made the process of siting hazardous waste facilities in California just as inequitable as it had been before the passage of the act. Formalism prevailed, but no new facilities have been sited. (154)

Although all of the county plans were supposed to be approved by 1994, only thirty-five of them were approved by the deadline. There was no movement within the legislature to continue the program or to provide funds for the counties to produce the plans and for the state to approve them.[26] Because DHS's implementation of the Hazardous Waste Management Act created such a controversy and essentially dismantled the Yimby initiative, there is little evidence to date about its effectiveness as a waste management strategy.[27]

Canada's siting of two hazardous waste facilities, first in Alberta and then in Manitoba, used many of the Yimby principles (see Rabe 1994). Although the siting approach used in these provinces was not as bottom-up as the California proposal, it captured many of the key features of Yimby, like early involvement of citizens, significant waste reduction programs, an integrated approach to waste management, and public education about waste issues. But according to Rabe (1994), particularly in the Alberta case, burden sharing was seen as critical to the success of the siting strategy because it meant that residents of Swan Hills would not feel that they were bearing the full burden of the province's waste generation. The siting effort included a regional system of collection and storage before the waste was transferred to Swan Hills. In addition, public officials were able to restrict the import of waste from other provinces, and this reassured the residents of Swan Hills that they would not be the nation's dumping ground but instead key participants in the management of Alberta's waste. Interestingly, although Minnesota state officials modeled their siting effort after that of Alberta, they never effectively incorporated ideas like fair share and burden sharing into their own siting plan.[28]

In several states, Minnesota among them, policymakers have tried to implement plans similar to Yimby for solid waste management. These too seemed promising at the outset but encountered problems as they were implemented. The central difficulty to overcome in this area was flow control. These solid waste plans were designed to get counties to cooperate in their management of waste and help them build regional disposal facilities to handle several counties' waste. However, to keep these facilities running at capacity, ordinances were passed that require waste produced in the cooperating counties to be sent to the new facilities. These flow control laws were challenged in a 1994 case, *Carbone v. the City of Clarkstown,* and the Supreme Court struck down such statutes on the grounds that they violate the commerce clause. In Minnesota the absence of flow control regulations forced a regional composting facility built by the East Central Solid Waste Commission to shut down because it was operating significantly below its capacity (Craggs 1995). Thus the lessons from California and from solid waste management indicate that there are still a number of significant legal and bureaucratic obstacles to the effective implementation of Yimby or fair share policies.

## Conclusion

Despite laments that citizens can too easily influence hazardous waste decisions, this study of Minnesota reveals that the path to citizen control is a difficult one. Among the obstacles that must be confronted are elite interest groups who can bargain and negotiate with state officials, legislators who are at times unaware of the impact of policies on their constituents, and state officials with a technical understanding of good policy and a desire to use that understanding as the basis of decision-making. In addition, at each turn citizens are faced with decision-makers who often view them as a nuisance in the policymaking arena and rarely see them as contributing to effective policymaking. The opinions that they hold are often disparaged as narrow, parochial, uninformed, or emotional. Not only are public officials skeptical of citizens' policy preferences, but they see citizens' opinions as something that they have a responsibility to change. From state officials' perspectives, only when citizens' views are consistent with state officials' understanding of the problem and the solution can "good" policies can be enacted. Given these obstacles, it is somewhat miraculous that citizens are able to influence policymaking at all.

But through persistence, resistance, research, mobilization, and strategic thinking, citizens can prevail to some extent. In this case it was the citizens' ability to repeatedly veto the state's policy initiatives that eventually gave them influence over hazardous waste policy. The ability of citizens to curtail the state's capacity when faced with both the state's coercive and non-coercive powers demonstrates that citizens can exercise some measure of control over policymakers, but that this political control is limited in important ways. Even though Minnesota citizens could block state initiatives and create a stalemate, they had little impact on the ability of the state to autonomously develop and pursue plans to which the citizens were opposed.

Most important, this case demonstrates that a process in which citizens influence policy is desirable. It is desirable not only to provide legitimacy to democratic governance, but it can be justified on the more difficult grounds of good policymaking. A deliberative and at times adversarial process requires all participants (both experts and citizens) to justify their technical assumptions and implicit and explicit value judgments. Although this process may be unwieldy and drawn out, this study shows that the alternative—insulated, technical decision-making—is what we should fear.

Democratic decision-making should be seen as part of the solution to managing complex social issues, not as part of the problem.

## Notes

1. See the introduction to Chapter 4 for further development of this debate.

2. Quoted in *democracy*, 1981, no. 1, 61.

3. Dean Rebuffoni, "Business Lobby Urged to Ask Its Members to Cut Pollution," *Star Tribune*, 6 February 1990, 8a. Interestingly, this bill was given little attention by the news media that covered the Red Lake Falls area, and the bill did not enter into debates about the need for the facility during the referendum in Red Lake Falls.

4. Gene Merriam, retired state senator, interview with author, St. Paul, Minnesota, 16 June 1998.

5. Minnesota Office of Environmental Assistance, 1992, *Hazardous Waste Capacity Assurance Plan*, St. Paul, Minnesota, 1.

6. Minnesota Office of Environmental Assistance, 1998, *1998 Pollution Prevention Evaluation Report*, St. Paul, Minnesota, 9.

7. Minnesota Office of Environmental Assistance, 1992, *Hazardous Waste Capacity Assurance Plan*, St. Paul, Minnesota, 5.

8. Minnesota Office of Environmental Assistance, 1998, *1998 Pollution Prevention Evaluation Report*, St. Paul, Minnesota, 14.

9. Most hazardous waste in Minnesota and elsewhere is handled on-site. In Minnesota companies that are required to file a Toxic Release Inventory (this includes most of "the major waste users, generators, and releasers of toxic pollutants") recycle 60 percent of their waste on-site. (Minnesota Office of Environmental Assistance 1998).

10. Minnesota Office of Environmental Assistance, 1997, *Manifested Shipments of Hazardous Waste by Minnesota Generators, 1992–1996*, St. Paul, Minnesota. These calculations exclude waste generated from clean-ups.

These figures can be somewhat misleading, since a reduction in waste sent to a landfill could occur because more waste stays on the site where it is produced. To see the effectiveness of waste reduction, it would be useful to have data on the total amount of waste generated in Minnesota. In its biennial report to the EPA Minnesota reported the following data for total waste generated in tons: 3,705,295 (1989); 6,384,145 (1991); 7,435,285 (1993); 1,584,675 (1995). Unfortunately, these data are the best available estimates but are not accurate because two large Minnesota companies were over-reporting their waste until 1995, when the problem was corrected.

11. Minnesota Office of Environmental Assistance, 1997, *Manifested Shipments of Hazardous Waste by Minnesota Generators 1992–1996*, St. Paul, Minnesota, 15.

12. Minnesota Office of Environmental Assistance, 1992, *Report on Hazardous and Industrial Waste Program*, St. Paul, Minnesota.

13. Minnesota Office of Environmental Assistance, 1994, *Hazardous and Nonhazardous Industrial Waste Programs: Evaluation Report,* St. Paul, Minnesota. According to one state official, the US Filter plant was sited without much public opposition because disposal is a much more controversial issue for the public than treatment is. The Rosemount plant does not take materials listed as hazardous waste, and this appears to have facilitated its siting.

14. Anonymous Minnesota official, interview with author, St. Paul, Minnesota, June 1998.

15. Minnesota Office of Enviromental Assistance, 1994, *Hazardous and Nonhazardous Industrial Waste Program,* St. Paul, Minnesota 5.

16. Ibid., 4. A consultant's report published in December 1990 came to a similar conclusion that the facility was not economically viable. If the state included "intangible benefits," like the long-term security that the facility might offer to Minnesota businesses, then the costs might be justified. However, " . . . the straight financial evaluation under certain assumptions shows it [the state] may not recover all of the capital and operating costs." (Dames and Moore 1990, 22)

17. Sue Boyle, resident of Koochiching County, interview with author, International Falls, Minnesota, 26 September 1989.

18. Mansbridge further elaborates this point in arguing:

> If a central goal of politics is to come to understand one's interests better, self-interest must have a legitimate role in the body politic. . . . Awakened, conscious adults must be able to understand their interests and negotiate for them in moments of conflict in ways that would not be possible in a culture that prescribed only "a disinterested attachment to the public good, exclusive and independent of all private and selfish interest." (Mansbridge 1990, 22)

This idea that the common good is arrived at through deliberation is also developed explicitly in Fishkin (1995).

19. For a more detailed discussion, see Lindblom (1990, Chapter 12) and Dahl (1989, Chapter 5).

20. Minnesota's movement toward pollution reduction also is not solely explained by its reputation as a liberal state with a culture that is generally supportive of government problem-solving, since it was led by a Republican governor while these reforms were undertaken. Thus this trend toward waste reduction is not limited to state governments controlled by liberal Democrats.

21. Most states have passed some sort of toxic reduction legislation, but Minnesota appears to be among the leaders in this area.

22. For details of California's attempt to cope with its hazardous waste problem using this strategy, see Mazmanian et al. (1988), Morell (1987, 1996), and Mazmanian and Morell (1992). Gerrard (1994) notes that New York and Michigan have incorporated plans for "internal geographic equity" (i.e., that regions share the burden for disposal according to their contribution to the problem) into state laws for siting (84 and note 115).

23. A strategy similar to this was proposed at a National Workshop on Facility Siting and is described in Kunreuther, Fitzgerald, and Aarts (1993).

24. In some ways this strategy mirrors the program developed by the EPA when they pushed responsibility down to the state level. However, as this case study suggests, trying to conduct siting at the state level still creates a sense of inequity and unwanted risk by those living near the site. By pushing the siting to the local level, citizens get more of a sense that everyone is doing their part rather than some communities assuming all or most of the burden.

25. Although these claims about the difficulty of getting citizens involved in preliminary policy discussion may be true, it is important to note that when statewide discussion about siting began in Minnesota, more than 2,000 people participated.

26. Gunther Moskat, Department of Toxic Substances Control, interview with author, 9 October 1998.

27. The state moved responsibility for approval of these plans to the Department of Toxic Substances Control in 1991. This facilitated the approval of some of the plans, but it was not enough to rescue the program.

28. As Rabe (1994) notes, Minnesota policymakers missed other key features in the Alberta plan. In addition to omitting burden sharing, they did not provide a comprehensive public education campaign across the state before the counties volunteered, nor did they stress waste reduction as part of an integrated waste management plan.

# Appendix A

The surveys of Red Lake and Koochiching Counties were conducted by the Minnesota Center for Survey Research at the University of Minnesota. The data were collected through two random-sample mail surveys sent to residents of Koochiching and Red Lake Counties. In Koochiching County 650 households were drawn at random and sent a survey. Three hundred seventy surveys were returned, yielding a response rate of 57 percent. In Red Lake 550 surveys were mailed to county residents. Three hundred thirty-seven surveys were returned, yielding a response rate of 61 percent. The Koochiching survey was conducted from 6 April to 11 May 1990. The Red Lake survey was conducted from 31 May to 6 July 1990.

It is important to note that these were slightly different survey settings. Red Lake County was in the midst of deciding whether to accept or reject the facility at the time the survey was administered. The county board of Koochiching County decided to withdraw the county as a potential host for the facility in March 1989, approximately a year before the survey was administered. Despite these differences, the survey results from the two counties are remarkably similar.

To validate that the surveys were representative of the two counties, I compared the survey results to census data on education and income for each. In Red Lake County census data showed that the average household income was $19,926 and that 64.3 percent of citizens were high school graduates. The survey results for income were collected using an ordinal scale, and the average income was $15–20,000. The percentage of high school graduates in the survey was 65.5 percent.

In Koochiching County the average household income from the census was $23,400, and 73 percent were high school graduates. The results from the survey show an average household income of $20–25,000 and 65 percent of respondents were high school graduates. In Koochiching there was a slightly higher percentage of respondents with college degrees than in the census data (13 percent in the sample and 10 percent in the population). Overall, there was a slightly higher education level in the sample than in the population for Koochiching but little or no difference in income.

One final point about the validity of the survey is that in Red Lake County a referendum was held on the facility in November 1990, and it was voted down with 65 percent opposing and 35 percent approving. As the results in Table 4.1 show, 65 percent of the survey respondents opposed the facility, 26.7 percent approved of it, and 8.3 percent were undecided. The results from the survey very closely match the referendum results.

At the end of the surveys for both counties an open-response section was available. Some of the information reported in this book is taken from these anonymous responses.

# Appendix B

facility    Think back to when the county was deciding whether or not the hazardous waste facility should be built in Koochiching. Did you favor or oppose the building of the facility?

fnecess    The facility is necessary for the State of Minnesota to meet its long-term goals of a clean environment.

frm    Building a hazardous waste facility in Red Lake will hurt the farm economy.

just-fac    There is not enough hazardous waste produced in our state to justify building this facility in Minnesota.

money    The money that the state was going to give the county was fair payment for allowing the state to build the facility in Northome/Red Lake County.

nowfac    The state should continue looking for a county to take the facility because Minnesota needs this facility.

prop    Locating the facility in Koochiching County/Red Lake County would have hurt property values.

| tech | On technical issues like the disposal of hazardous waste, I trust the state to look out for my best interest and the interest of Minnesota. |
|---|---|
| tour | Building a hazardous waste treatment plant in Koochiching County would have hurt tourism in the county. |
| transp | The chance of hazardous waste accidentally spilling during transport to the treatment facility is small. |
| twins | The state should build a facility closer to the Twin Cities because that is where most of the hazardous waste is produced. |
| water | The chances of the hazardous waste facility polluting the ground water were high. |

## Trust Questions

Please indicate how much you *trust* the state to make good decisions on the following issues.

| ed | Educating our children |
|---|---|
| env | Protecting the environment |
| frm | Maintaining the farm economy |
| tax | Operating a fair tax system |
| wlf | Providing welfare payments |

# Appendix C

The survey data used in this analysis do not meet the conventional distributional requirements for the measurement part of the covariance structure models, in which multivariate normality for both observed and latent variables is assumed. Generally, this assumption of normality is violated in the analysis of survey data in which the data are typically censored to be above zero and are often skewed. Because of the non-normality, the ordinal variables can also lead to heteroskedastic disturbances and therefore inefficient estimators of parameters.

In addition, the problem is compounded by the fact that the latent variables are assumed to be continuous variables, whereas the observed variables are ordinal. This problem grows more serious as the number of categories is reduced (the problem is small when the number of categories is greater than twelve) (Jöreskog and Sörbom 1989). The consequences for analysis of survey data are that "the covariance structure hypothesis holds for latent continuous indicators, but not for ordinal variables, where the standardized coefficient estimates appear to be attenuated" (Bollen 1989, 438).

The procedure for resolving these violations is twofold. First, the non-linear relationship between the continuous latent variables and the ordinal observed variables is estimated.

For $z^*$, the continuous latent variable thought to be influencing the observed variable z (ordinal variable = 1, 2, 3 . . .), there is a threshold effect $(a_i)$. The assumption is that once the latent variable $z^*$ crosses a threshold $(a_i)$, a new value for the ordinal variable will be observed (Bollen 1989, 439; Maddala 1983). The threshold levels are estimated and are used to relate the observed ordinal variable (z) to the latent continuous variable $(z^*)$. These continuous variables can then be correlated to get a matrix of polychoric correlations for utilization as the input for the covariance structure model.

However, this alone will not solve the problems encountered in the analysis of survey data, because the polychoric correlations will produce consistent estimates of coefficients but incorrect standard errors, chi-square tests, and other significant tests when estimated using the conventional maximum likelihood estimator. This is because the maximum likelihood estimator assumes a multivariate normal distribution. These problems with the maximum likelihood estimator can be overcome through the use of a weighted least-squares estimator, which is similar to the correction of heteroskedasticity in Ordinary Least Squares (OLS) estimation. The weighted least-squares estimator relies on the asymptotic covariance (ACOV) matrix and will provide asymptotically efficient estimators by allowing weaker distributional assumptions than multivariate normality allows. The difficulty is that estimating the ACOV matrix requires large samples to get reliable estimates (Jöreskog and Sörbom 1989). Fortunately, for the surveys of these two counties the sample size was large enough to estimate the ACOV matrix, if the number of variables in the models was kept down.

The models for these two counties were estimated using LISREL 7, with the ACOV matrix estimated using the PRELIS preprocessor program.

# Bibliography

## Books and Journal Articles

Almond, Gabriel. 1988. "The Return to the State." *American Political Science Review* 82:3, 853–873.

Andrews, Richard N. 1988. "Hazardous Waste Facility Siting: State Approaches," in *Dimensions of Hazardous Waste Politics and Policy,* eds. C. Davis and J. P. Lester. New York: Greenwood Press, 117–128.

Arendt, Hannah. 1977. *The Life of the Mind.* New York: Harcourt Brace Jovanovich.

Barber, Benjamin. 1984. *Strong Democracy: Participatory Politics for a New Age.* Berkeley: University of California Press.

Beckman, Peter. 1973. *Eco-Hysterics and the Technophobes.* Boulder, CO: Golem.

Beetham, David. 1987. *Bureaucracy.* Minneapolis: University of Minnesota Press.

Bentler, P. M. 1980. "Multivariate Analysis with Latent Variables: Causal Modeling." *Annual Review of Psychology,* 419–456.

Bentley, Arthur. 1908. *The Process of Government.* Chicago: University of Chicago Press.

Berelson, Bernard. 1952. "Democratic Theory and Public Opinion." *Public Opinion Quarterly* 16, 313–330.

Berry, Frances S., and William D. Berry. 1990. "State Lottery Adoptions as Policy Innovations: An Event History Analysis." *American Political Science Review* 84, 395–415.

Bollen, Kenneth A. 1989. *Structural Equations with Latent Variables.* New York: Wiley-Interscience.

Bowman, Ann O'M., and Richard Kearney. 1986. *The Resurgence of the States.* Englewood Cliffs, NJ: Prentice-Hall.

Breyer, Stephen G. 1993. *Breaking The Vicious Circle: Toward Effective Risk Regulation.* Cambridge: Harvard University Press.

Carter, Luther J. 1987. *Nuclear Imperative and Public Trust: Dealing with Radioactive Waste.* Washington, D.C.: Resources for the Future.

Carter, Luther J., and Thomas H. Pigford. 1998. "Getting Yucca Mountain Right." *Bulletin of Atomic Scientists* 54, 56–62.

*Corporate report.* 1991. Edina: Corporate Report, Inc.

*Corporate Report Fact Book.* 1992. Minneapolis: MCP, Inc.

Craggs, Robert. 1995. "Regionalization: A Solid Waste Solution." *American City and County* 110:9, 44–51.

Cronin, Thomas E. 1989. *Direct Democracy: The Politics of Initiative, Referendum, and Recall.* Cambridge: Harvard University Press.

Cvetkovich, George, and Timothy C. Earle. 1992. "Environmental Hazards and the Public." *Journal of Social Issues* 48:4, 1–20.

Dahl, Robert. 1956. *A Preface to Democratic Theory.* Chicago: University of Chicago Press.

———. 1961. *Who Governs: Democracy and Power in an American City.* New Haven: Yale University Press.

———. 1985. *Controlling Nuclear Weapons: Democracy versus Guardianship.* Syracuse: Syracuse University Press.

———. 1989. *Democracy and Its Critics.* New Haven: Yale University Press.

Davis, Charles E. 1984–1985. "Substance and Procedure in Hazardous Waste Facility Siting." *Journal of Environmental Systems* 14:1, 51–62.

Davis, Charles, and James P. Lester. 1986. "Public Involvement in Hazardous Waste Facility Siting Decisions." *Polity* 19:2, 296–304.

———. 1988. "Hazardous Waste Politics and the Policy Process," in *Dimensions of Hazardous Waste Politics and Policy,* eds. C. Davis and J. P. Lester. New York: Greenwood Press, 1–37.

Delli-Carpini, Michael X., and Scott Keeter. 1996. *What Americans Know about Politics and Why It Matters.* New Haven: Yale University Press.

Downs, Anthony. 1967. *Inside Bureaucracy.* Boston: Little, Brown.

Dryzek, John. 1987. *Rational Ecology: Environment and Political Economy.* New York: Basil Blackwell.

———. 1988. "Mismeasuring Political Man." *Journal of Politics* 50:3, 705–726.

Elazar, Daniel J. 1984. *American Federalism: A View from the States,* 3rd edition. New York: Harper and Row.

Elliot, Michael L. P. 1984. "Improving Community Acceptance of Hazardous Waste Facilities Through Alternative Systems for Mitigating and Managing Systems." *Hazardous Waste* 3, 397–410.

Erikson, Robert S., Gerald C. Wright, and John P. McIver. 1993. *Statehouse Democracy: Public Opinion and Policy in the American States.* New York: Cambridge University Press.

Feldman, David, and Ruth Anne Hanahan. Forthcoming. "Environmental Priority-Setting Through Comparative Risk Assessment." *Environmental Management.*

Fenno, Richard. 1973. *Congressmen in Committees.* Boston: Little, Brown.

Fishkin, James S. 1995. *The Voice of the People: Public Opinion and Democracy.* New Haven: Yale University Press.

Freudenburg, William R., and Susan K. Pastor. 1992. "Nimbys and Lulus: Stalking the Syndromes." *Journal of Social Issues* 48:4, 39–61.

Frey, Bruno S., and Felix Oberholzer-Gee. 1996. "Fair Siting Procedures: An Empirical Analysis of Their Importance and Characteristics." *Journal of Policy Analysis and Management* 15:3, 353–376.

Frey, Bruno S., Felix Oberholzer-Gee, and Reiner Eichenberger. 1996. "The Old Lady Visits Your Backyard: A Tale of Morals and Markets." *Journal of Political Economy* 104:6, 1297–1313.

Gerrard, Michael B. 1994. *Whose Backyard, Whose Risk: Fear and Fairness in Toxic and Nuclear Siting.* Cambridge: MIT Press.

Gormley, William T. 1989. *Taming the Bureaucracy: Muscles, Prayers, and Other Strategies.* Princeton: Princeton University Press.

———. 1991. "The Bureaucracy and Its Masters: The New Madisonian System in the US." *Governance* 4:1, 1–18.

Gray, Virginia. 1973. "Innovation in the States: A Diffusion Study." *American Political Science Review* 67, 1174–1185.

Greenberg, Michael R. 1984. *Hazardous Waste Sites: The Credibility Gap.* Rutgers, NJ: Center for Urban Policy Research.

Hadden, Susan G., Joan Veillette, and Thomas Brandt. 1983. "State Roles in Siting Hazardous Waste Disposal Facilities: From State Preemption to Local Veto," in *The Politics of Hazardous Waste Management,* eds. James P. Lester and Ann O'M. Bowman. Durham, NC: Duke University Press.

Hall, Bob, and Mary Lee Kerr. 1991–1992. *Green Index: A State-by-State Guide to the Nation's Environmental Health.* Washington, D.C.: Island Press.

Hamilton, Lawrence C. 1985. "Concern about Toxic Wastes: Three Demographic Predictors." *Sociological Perspectives* 28, 463–486.

Heclo, Hugh. 1974. *Modern Social Politics in Britain and Sweden.* New Haven: Yale University Press.

Hovey, Kendra A. and Harold A. Hovey. 1998. *Congressional Quarterly's State Fact Finder.* Washington, D.C.: Congressional Quarterly, Inc.

Hunter, Susan, and Kevin M. Leyden. 1995. "Beyond Nimby: Explaining Opposition to Hazardous Waste Facilities." *Policy Studies Journal* 23:4, 601–619.

Ikenberry, John. 1988. "Conclusion: An Institutional Approach to American Foreign Economic Policy." *International Organization* 42, 219–243.

Inhaber, Herbert. 1998. *Slaying the NIMBY Dragon.* New Brunswick: Transaction.

Jöreskog, Karl G., and Dag Sörbom. 1989. *LISREL 7: User's Reference Manual.* Mooresville, IN: Scientific Software.

Keech, William R. 1995. *Economic Politics: The Costs of Democracy.* Cambridge: Cambridge University Press.

Kraft, Michael E., and Bruce B. Clary. 1991. "Citizen Participation and the NIMBY Syndrome: Public Responses to Radioactive Waste Disposal." *Western Political Quarterly* 44:2, 299–328.

Krasner, Stephen. 1978. *Defending the National Interest: Raw Material Investments and U.S. Foreign Policy.* Princeton: Princeton University Press.

Krause, George. 1996. "The Institutional Dynamics of Policy Administration: Bureaucratic Influence over Securities Regulation." *American Journal of Political Science* 40:4, 1083–1121.

Kunreuther, Howard, Kevin Fitzgerald, and Thomas D. Aarts. 1993. "Siting Noxious Facilities: A Test of the Facilities Siting Credo." *Risk Analysis* 13, 301–318.

Kunreuther, Howard, and Paul Slovic. 1996. "Science, Values, and Risk." *The Annals of the American Academy of Political and Social Science* 545, 116–125.

Lake, Robert W. 1993. "Rethinking NIMBY." *Journal of the American Planning Association* 59:1, 87–93.

Leiss, William. 1996. "Three Phases in the Evolution of Risk Communication Practice." *Annals of the American Academy of Political and Social Science* 545, 85–94.

Lester, James P. 1994. "A New Federalism? Environmental Policy in the States," in *Environmental Policy in the 1990's,* eds. Norman J. Vig and Michael E. Kraft. Washington, D.C.: CQ Press.

Lester, James P., James Franke, Ann O'M. Bowman, and Kenneth Kramer. 1983. "Hazardous Wastes, Politics, and Public Policy: A Comparative State Analysis." *Western Political Quarterly* 36:2, 257–285.

Lindblom, Charles. 1965. *The Intelligence of Democracy.* New York: Free Press.

———. 1977. *Politics and Markets.* New York: Basic Books.

———. 1982. "The Market as Prison." *Journal of Politics* 44, 324–326.

———. 1990. *Inquiry and Change.* New Haven: Yale University Press.

Lindblom, Charles, and Edward J. Woodhouse. 1993. *The Policy-Making Process,* 3rd edition. Englewood Cliffs, NJ: Prentice-Hall.

Lowi, Theodore. 1979. *The End of Liberalism.* New York: W. W. Norton.

———. 1988. "The Return to the State: Critiques." *American Political Science Review* 82:3, 875–891.

Maddala, G. S. 1983. *Limited-Dependent and Qualitative Variables in Econometrics.* Cambridge: Cambridge University Press.

Mansbridge, Jane J. 1990. "The Rise and Fall of Self-Interest in the Explanation of Political Life," in *Beyond Self-Interest,* ed. Jane J. Mansbridge. Chicago: Chicago University Press, 3–24.

Margolis, Howard. 1996. *Dealing with Risk: Why the Public and the Experts Disagree on Environmental Issues.* Chicago: University of Chicago Press.

Matheny, Albert R., and Bruce A. Williams. 1988. "Rethinking Participation: Assessing Florida's Strategy for Siting Hazardous Waste Disposal Facilities," in *Dimensions of Hazardous Waste Politics and Policy,* eds. C. Davis and J. P. Lester. New York: Greenwood Press, 37–52.

Mazmanian, Daniel, and David Morell. 1990. "The NIMBY Syndrome: Facility Siting and the Failure of Democratic Discourse," in *Environmental Policy in the 1990s,* eds. Norman J. Vig and Michael Kraft. Washington, D.C.: CQ Press.

———. 1992. *Beyond Superfailure: America's Toxic Policies for the 1990s.* Boulder, CO: Westview.

Mazmanian, Daniel, Michael Stanley-Jones, and Miriam J. Green. 1988. *Breaking Political Deadlock: California's Experiment in Public-Private Cooperation on Hazardous Waste Policy.* Claremont, CA: California Institute of Public Affairs.

McCubbins, Matthew D., and Thomas Schwartz. 1984. "Congressional Oversight Overlooked: Police Patrol and Fire Alarms." *American Journal of Political Science* 28:1, 165–179.

Miller, Jon D. 1987. "Scientifically Illiterate." *American Demographics* 9:6, 26–32.

Mintrom, Michael. 1997. "Policy Entreprenuers and the Diffusion of Innovation." *American Journal of Political Science* 41, 738–770.

Moe, Terry M. 1984. "The New Economics of Organization." *American Journal of Political Science* 28:4, 739–777.

Morell, David. 1984. "Siting and the Politics of Equity." *Hazardous Waste* 1, 555–571.

———. 1987. "Siting and the Politics of Equity," in *Resolving Locational Conflict,* ed. Robert W. Lake. New Brunswick, NJ: Center for Urban Policy Research, 117–136.

———. 1996. "Hazardous Waste Management and Facility Siting in California," in *Hazardous Waste Siting and Democratic Choice,* ed. Donald Munton. Washington, D.C.: Georgetown University Press, 142–180.

Morell, David L., and Christopher Magorian. 1982. *Siting Hazardous Waste Facilities.* Cambridge, MA: Ballinger.

Munton, Donald. 1996. "The Nimby Phenomenon and Approaches to Facility Siting," in *Hazardous Waste Siting and Democratic Choice,* ed. Donald Munton. Washington, D.C.: Georgetown University Press, 1–53.

Nordlinger, Eric. 1981. *On the Autonomy of the Democratic State.* Cambridge: Harvard University Press.

———. 1988. "The Return to the State: Critiques." *American Political Science Review* 82:3, 875–891.

Ochsner, Michele, and Caron Chess. 1996. "Pollution Prevention's Promise, Limits, and Relevance to Planners." *Journal of Planning Literature* 11:1, 5–20.

O'Hare, Michael. 1977. "Not on My Block You Don't: Facility Siting and the Strategic Importance of Compensation." *Public Policy* 25:4, 407–458.

O'Hare, Michael, Lawrence Bacow, and Debra Sanderson. 1983. *Facility Siting.* New York: Van Nostrand.

Ophuls, William. 1977. *Ecology and the Politics of Scarcity.* San Francisco: W. H. Freeman.

———. 1992. *Ecology and the Politics of Scarcity Revisited: The Unraveling of the American Dream.* New York: W. H. Freeman.

Orloff, Ann, and Theda Skocpol. 1984. "Why Not Equal Protection? Explaining the Politics of Public Social Policy Spending in Britain, 1900–1911, and the United States, 1880s–1920." *American Sociological Review* 49, 726–750.

Page, Benjamin. 1996. *Who Deliberates.* Chicago: University of Chicago Press.

Page, Benjamin I., and Robert Y. Shapiro. 1992. *The Rational Public: Fifty Years of Trends in Americans' Policy Preferences.* Chicago: University of Chicago Press.

Piller, Charles. 1991. *The Fail-Safe Society: Community Defiance and the End of American Technological Optimism.* New York: Basic Books.

Pitkin, Hanna Fenichel. 1967. *The Concept of Representation.* Berkeley: University of California Press.

Portney, Kent E. 1988. "The Effect of Economics in Lay Perceptions of Risk," in *Dimensions of Hazardous Waste Politics and Policy,* eds. C. Davis and J. P. Lester. New York: Greenwood Press, 54–62.

———. 1991. *Siting Hazardous Waste Treatment Facilities: The Nimby Syndrome.* New York: Auburn House.

Press, Daniel. 1994. *Democratic Dilemmas in the Age of Ecology.* Durham, NC: Duke University Press.

Rabe, Barry. 1994. *Beyond Nimby: Hazardous Waste Siting in Canada and the United States.* Washington, D.C.: Brookings Institution.

Reinke, Dan. 1988. "Development of a Stabilization and Containment Facility in Minnesota." Paper presented at the 81st Annual Meeting of the Air Pollution Control Association, Dallas, TX.

Rosenbaum, Walter. 1983. "The Politics of Public Participation in Hazardous Waste Management," in *The Politics of Hazardous Waste Management,* eds. James P. Lester and Ann O'M. Bowman. Durham, NC: Duke University Press.

Rowland, C. K., and Linda Walton. 1983. "Producer Concentration and Hazardous Waste Regulation: An Interstate Comparison." Paper presented at the 1983 Annual Meeting of the American Political Science Association.

Samdahl, Diane, and Robert Robertson. 1989. "Social Determinants of Environmental Concern: Specification and Test of the Model." *Environment and Behavior* 21:1, 57–81.

Schneider, Mark, and Paul Teske, with Michael Mintrom. 1995. *Public Entreprenuers: Agents for Change in American Government.* Princeton: Princeton University Press.

Schumpeter, Joseph A. 1947. *Capitalism, Socialism, and Democracy.* New York: Harper and Bros.

Skocpol, Theda. 1980. "Political Response to Capitalist Crisis: Neo-Marxist Theories of the State." *Politics and Society* 10, 155–201.

———. 1985. "Bringing the State Back In: Strategies of Analysis in Current Research," in *Bringing the State Back In,* eds. Peter Evans, Dietrich Reuschemeyer, and Theda Skocpol. New York: Cambridge University Press, 3–43.

Skocpol, Theda, and Kenneth Finegold. 1982. "State Capacity and Economic Intervention in the Early New Deal." *Political Science Quarterly* 97:2, 255–277.

Skowronek, Stephen. 1982. *Building the New American State.* Cambridge: Cambridge University Press.

Slovic, Paul, Baruch Fischhoff, and Sarah Lichtenstein. 1982. "Facts and Fears: Understanding the Perceived Risk," in *Judgment under Uncertainty: Heuristics and Biases,* eds. Daniel Kahneman, Paul Slovic, and Amos Tversky. Cambridge: Cambridge University Press.

Szasz, Andrew. 1994. *Ecopopulism: Toxic Waste and the Movement for Environmental Justice.* Minneapolis: University of Minnesota Press.

Tocqueville, Alexis de. 1969. *Democracy in America.* Garden City, NY: Doubleday.

Truman, David. 1951. *The Governmental Process.* New York: Knopf.

Walker, Jack L. 1969. "The Diffusion of Innovations among the American States." *American Political Science Review* 63, 880–899.

Weber, Max. 1946. "Essay on Bureaucracy," *From Max Weber: Essays in Sociology.* Translated, edited, and with an introduction, by H. H. Gerth and C. Wright Mills. New York: Oxford University Press.

Weissberg, Robert. 1976. *Public Opinion and Popular Government.* Englewood Cliffs, NJ: Prentice-Hall.

Williams, Bruce A., and Albert R. Matheny. 1995. *Democracy, Dialogue, and Environmental Disputes: The Contested Languages of Social Regulation.* New Haven: Yale University Press.

Wilson, James Q. 1980. *The Politics of Regulation.* New York: Basic Books.

Wood, B. Dan. 1988. "Principals, Bureaucrats, and Responsiveness in Clean-Air Enforcements." *American Political Science Review* 82:1, 214–234.

Wood, B. Dan and Richard W. Waterman. 1991. "The Dynamics of Political Control of the Bureaucracy," *American Political Science Review* 85:3, 801–828.

Wolley, John. 1984. *Monetary Politics: The Federal Reserve and the Politics of Monetary Policy.* New York: Cambridge University Press.

## Public Documents

Cerrell and Associates. 1984. Report prepared for the California Waste Management Board.

Dames and Moore. 1990. *Economic Review of a Proposed Stabilization and Containment Facility.* Prepared by Capsule Environmental Engineering, St. Paul, MN.

Ditmore, Jack. 10 April 1989. Memorandum, Minnesota Environmental Quality Board.

Ford, Kenneth G., Corporate Manager, Environmental Affairs, Honeywell Corporation. Letter to Richard Dunn, Chair of the Waste Management Board, 17 January 1984. Waste Management Board Records, State Historical Archives, Minnesota Historical Society.

Johnson, Tom, Legislative Liaison. 23 August 1988. Memorandum to Waste Management Board staff.

"Koochiching County Contract." 1989. Koochiching County, MN.

Minnesota Waste Management Board. 1981. *Charting a Course: Public Participation in the Siting of Hazardous Waste Facilities.* Crystal, MN.

Minnesota Waste Management Board. 1984a. *Draft Certificate of Need.* St. Paul, MN.

Minnesota Waste Management Board. 1984b. Report on the 16 January 1984 Public Hearing on the Waste Management Board's *Draft Hazardous Waste Management Plan and Certificate of Need.* Waste Management Board Records, State Historical Archives, Minnesota Historical Society.

Minnesota Waste Management Board. 1988. *Stabilization and Containment: Report on Facility Development.* St. Paul, MN.

Minnesota Waste Management Board. 26 May 1988. Minutes. Crystal, MN.

Minnesota Waste Management Board. 16 September 1988. Minutes of the Hazardous Waste Planning Council. St. Paul, MN.

Minnesota Waste Management Board. 1989. *Capacity Assurance Plan.* St. Paul, MN.

Minnesota Office of Environmental Assistance. 1992. *Hazardous Waste Capacity Assurance Plan.* St. Paul, MN.

Minnesota Office of Environmental Assistance. 1994. *Hazardous and Nonhazardous Industrial Waste Programs: Evaluation Report.* St. Paul, MN.

Morely, John, Waste Management Board staff member. 4 August 1988. Memorandum to Dennis Taylor, Administrative Manager.

Pavelich, Joseph, Chair of Waste Management Board. 1989. Response to *Waste Management Board Financial and Compliance Audit for the Period July 1, 1985 through October 7, 1988.* Office of the Legislative Auditor, Financial Audit Division, St. Paul, MN.

Port, Terri Ann, Director of Facility Development of Waste Management Board. 20 October 1988. Letter to Jody Gross, opponent of facility development in Koochiching County.

Port, Terri Ann, Director of Facility Development of Waste Management Board. 3 March 1989. "Summary of Issues Regarding Facility Development Program." Memorandum to Hazardous Waste Planning Council.

Office of the Legislative Auditor, Financial Audit Division. 1989. *Waste Management Board Financial and Compliance Audit for the Period July 1, 1985 through October 7, 1988,* St. Paul, MN.

Shuster, Dan, President of Metro Recovery Systems. 20 January 1989. Letter to Senator Robert Lessard.

United States Department of Commerce. 1990. *Statistical Abstract of the United States.* Washington, D.C.: U.S. Dept. of Commerce, Social and Economic Statistics Administration, Bureau of the Census.

United States Environmental Protection Agency. 1979. *Siting of Hazardous Waste Management Facilities and Public Opposition: Final Report.* Report prepared by Centaur Associates, Inc.

Waste Management Act, 1980. (MN 155A.193).

## Newspaper Articles

Beager, Laurel. "Group Sees Waste Site as Environmental Responsibility." *Northome Record,* 15 November 1988, 1.

Beager, Laurel, and Tom Klein. "MRS Sees State as Competition." *Daily Journal,* 1 March 1989.

Broad, William J. "A Mountain of Trouble." *New York Times Magazine.* 18 November 1990, 37–40.

"Citizens at Northome Waste Meeting Express Opposition to Hazardous Waste Site." *Littlefork Times,* 3 August 1988.

Glaberson, William. "Coping in the Age of Nimby." *New York Times.* 19 June 1988, sec. 3, 1.

Gross, Jody. Letter to the Editor. *International Falls Journal,* 28 April 1988, 13.

"Hale Approves Partial Closing of the Waste Management Board Records." *Northome Record,* 9 August 1988.

Hanson, Bernie. Letter to the Editor. *International Falls Journal,* 3 May 1988, 7.

"Hazardous Waste Advisory Council Tours Site in Alberta." *Littlefork Times,* 14 October 1987.

"Hazardous Waste Contract." *Red Lake Falls Gazette,* 10 October 1990.

Interview with Chuck Dayton, Sierra Club Lobbyist. *Sierra North Star,* June 1980, 3.

Lindeke, Dennis. "The Hazardous Waste Problem in Minnesota." *Sierra North Star,* February 1981, 7.

Linder, Rita, and Steven Linder. Letter to the Editor. *Oklee Herald,* 18 May 1988.

"List of Counties in WMB Site Search Trimmed Down to Eight." *Red Lake Falls Gazette,* 25 November 1987.

*Northome Record.* Item on Joseph Pavelich, Chair of the Waste Management Board. 10 May 1988.

Oberdorfer, Dan. "Group Fighting to Keep Waste Site out of Carver County." *Minneapolis Star and Tribune,* 27 March 1983, 3B.

Rebuffoni, Dean. "Business Lobby Urged to Ask Its Members to Cut Pollution." *Minneapolis Star and Tribune,* 6 February 1990, 8A.

Rebuffoni, Dean, and Jim Dawson. "Proposals May End Search for Waste Dump in State." *Minneapolis Star and Tribune,* 16 March 1984, 3B.

Salisbury, Bill, and Allen Short. "Moratorium Set on Hazardous Waste Site Search." *St. Paul Pioneer,* 25 April 1984, 10A.

"Waste Management Board in Total Control." *Littlefork Times,* 18 May 1988.

Wilkerling, Bobbie. "Northome Commissioner Talks about His Role." *International Clipper Viewpoint,* 28 December 1988, 1.

———. "Koochiching Turns Down Hazardous Waste Facility." *Pioneer.* 22 March 1989, 1.

## *Interviews*

Bruce Biggins, Koochiching County Commissioner, interview with author, International Falls, Minnesota, 26 September 1989.

Susan Boyle, resident of Koochiching County, interview with author, International Falls, Minnesota, 26 September 1989.

Doris Hanson, Koochiching County Commissioner, interview with author, International Falls, Minnesota, 27 September 1989.

Diane Jensen, Clean Water Action Committee, interview with author, Minneapolis, Minnesota, 25 July 1990.

Dan Joyce, member of the Koochiching County advisory council, interview with author, Littlefork, Minnesota, 28 September 1989.

Dee Long, Minnesota State Representative, interview with author, St. Paul, Minnesota, 7 July 1990.

Bob Lowman, Preserve Our Land, telephone interview with author, 3 August 1990.

Gene Merriam, Minnesota State Senator, interview with author, St. Paul, Minnesota, 16 July 1990; telephone interview with author, St. Paul, Minnesota, 16 June 1998.

Neil Miller, Public Affairs Officer, Waste Management Board, interview with author, St. Paul, Minnesota, 29 April 1990.

Jean Moser, member of the Red Lake County advisory council, interview with author, Red Lake Falls, Minnesota, 10 April 1990.

Gunther Moskat, California Department of Toxic Substances Control, telephone interview with author, 9 October 1998.

Velma Oakland, resident of Red Lake County, interview with author, Red Lake Falls, Minnesota, 9 April 1990.

Sue Robertson, Legislative Assistant to the Legislative Commission on Waste Management, interview with author, St. Paul, Minnesota, 7 July 1990.

Don Sandbeck, Koochiching County Commissioner, interview with author, International Falls, Minnesota, 27 September 1989.

Ken Stabler, Acting Director of Facility Development, Waste Management Board, interview with author, Minneapolis, Minnesota, 20 June 1990.

Russ Susag, Environmental Officer 3M Corporation, interview with author, St. Paul, Minnesota, 30 June 1990.

Gene Ulring, County Engineer Red Lake County, interview with author, Red Lake Falls, Minnesota, 19 April 1990.

# Index

Hale, Sandra J., 70
Hazardous Waste Management
    Act (California), 139–140
hazardous waste policy
    citizen overall stance on, 92
    reduction versus disposal,
        35
    theoretical aspects of, 22–26
hazardous waste policy
    (Minnesota)
    citizen opposition, 27, 36–38
    first funding for siting, 26–27
    moratorium on siting process,
        38–42
    scope of analysis of, 14–16
    stabilization/containment
        facility alternative, 39–50
    and Toxic Pollution Prevention
        Act (TPPA), 129–130
    voluntary siting, 40–42,
        50–81
    and Waste Management Act,
        27–36
    See also Voluntary siting
heavy metals, 71, 130

information office, 75
interest groups, political theory of,
    22, 34
International Falls, 65
International Falls Journal, 68
International Technologies (IT),
    67

Johnson, Tom, 78
Joint Committee on Solid and
    Hazardous Waste, 27–28

Kemeny, John, 128
Koochiching County, Minnesota,
    12
    industry in, 65
    negotiation process, 69
    opposition groups, 66–68, 77, 80
    population of, 65
    survey results, 95, 104, 109–113
    See also Voluntary siting

Legislative Commission on Waste
    Management (LCWM), 31,
    37–38
legislative oversight, 38, 41
Linder, Ron, 101
Littlefork Times, 74
Long, Dee, 37, 41

McQuaid-Cook, Jennifer, 72, 77
market system, and policymaking,
    22–23
Media Rare, 72–73
media relations, 72–75
    importance of, 74–75
    state activities, 73–75
Merriam, Gene, 41
Metropolitan Waste Control
    Commission (MWCC), siting
    process, 26–27
Metro Recovery Systems (MRS),
    46–47, 131
Miller, Neil, 42, 44, 45, 48, 49
Minnesota
    counties of, 13
    See also Hazardous waste policy
        (Minnesota)
Minnesota COACT, 33